MENTAL PROPERTY AT THE BENEFIT OF COMPANIES

BILAISH KABEET

TABLE OF CONTENTS

WHY IS INTELLECTUAL PROPERTY RELEVANT TO YOUR SME?

Intellectual property, creativity and the spirit of invention surround us. Every product or service we use in our daily existence is the result of a long chain of innovations, big or small, such as changes in designs or improvements that make a product look or work. current. Let's take a simple product, such as a pen. Ladislao Biro's famous patented ballpoint pen is, in many respects, a capital discovery. But many others have, in turn, improved the product and its designs and legally protected their improvements by acquiring intellectual property rights. Your pen brand is also an intellectual property that helps the producer market the product and build customer loyalty.

And this will be the case with almost any product or service offered on the market. For example a compact disc player: it is likely that patent protection has been obtained for its various technical parts. Its design or model may be protected by industrial design rights. The company name is most likely protected by a trademark and the music played by the player is (or was) protected by copyright.

So what is the effect on your business?

No matter what product your company makes or what service it provides, it is likely to regularly use and create a large amount of intellectual property. However, you must always consider the measures required to protect, administer and enforce it in order to obtain the best possible commercial results from the ownership of its rights. If you use the intellectual property that belongs to others, then you should consider buying it or acquiring the rights to use it by taking out a license to avoid any litigation and the ensuing costs.

Almost all SMEs have a trade name or one or more trademarks and must think about protecting them. Most will hold valuable confidential business information, ranging from customer lists to sales methods that they would like to protect. Many will have developed original and creative designs. Many others will have produced, or helped to publish, broadcast or retail a copyrighted work. Some may have invented or improved a product or service.

In all such examples, your SME needs to consider how best to use the IP system to its own advantage. Intellectual property can help your SME in almost every aspect of growing your business and your competitive strategy: from development to product design, from providing services to marketing and obtaining financial resources for exporting or expanding your business overseas through licensing or franchising.

For all information on this subject and many others, you can consult the pages of this website and discover the world of intellectual property and the possibilities it offers to your SME.

HOW CAN INTELLECTUAL PROPERTY INCREASE THE MARKET VALUE OF YOUR SME?

Intellectual property is not always appreciated at its fair value and the prospects of future benefits it can offer are largely underestimated by SMEs. However, when IP is legally protected and there is market demand for IP-protected products or services, it can become a valuable business asset.

Intellectual property can create revenue for your SME through the licensing, sale, or marketing of protected products or services that can significantly improve the company's market share or increase its profit margins.

Intellectual property rights can increase the value of your SME in the eyes of investors and financing institutions.

During a sale, merger or acquisition, intellectual property assets can significantly enhance the value of your company and sometimes constitute the main, if not the only, real assets of value.

The strategic use of intellectual property assets can therefore significantly increase the competitiveness of your SME. Small and medium enterprises should ensure that they are up to the challenge and take steps to exploit their intellectual property and protect it as much as possible. Like tangible property, intellectual property assets must be acquired and maintained (see "Can your SME obtain and maintain intellectual property protection?"), accounted for, valued, duly verified and carefully managed to fully exploit them (see "How to manage your SME's intellectual property assets?"). But above all,

LINTELLECTUAL PROPERTY,A COMMERCIAL ASSET

A company's assets fall into two broad categories: tangible assets – including but not limited to buildings, machinery, financial assets and infrastructure – and intangible assets – which range from human capital and know-how to ideas, brand images, designs or models and other intangible results of a society's ability to create and innovate. Previously, the value of a company was based primarily on tangible assets which were believed to play a determining role in the competitiveness of a company in the market. In recent years, the situation has changed significantly. More and more, and mainly because of the revolution in information technology and the rise of the tertiary sector, companies are realizing that their intangible assets often acquire more value than their tangible assets.

In short, large warehouses and factories are being replaced by high-powered software and innovative ideas, the main sources of revenue for a large and growing proportion of businesses around the world. And even in sectors where traditional production techniques still dominate, continuous innovation and boundless creativity become the keys to increased competitiveness in tough domestic or international markets. As intangible assets now take a decisive turn, SMEs will have to find out how to make the best use of them.

The best way to do this is to legally protect intangibles and, where they meet the criterion for intellectual property protection, to acquire and maintain intellectual property rights. These rights may be acquired in particular for the following categories of intangible property:

Innovative products and processes (through patents and utility models);

Cultural, artistic and literary works, including, in most countries, computer software and data compilation (subject to copyright and related rights protection);

Creative designs, including textile designs (through industrial design rights);

Distinctive signs (mainly through trademark protection, including collective and certification marks, but in some cases through geographical indications; see below);

Semiconductor chips (with protection of layout designs or integrated circuit topographies);

Denominations of products of a certain quality or reputation attributable to geographical origin (subject to the protection of geographical indications); and

Trade secrets (with protection of undisclosed information of commercial value).

LA PROTECTION OF INTELLECTUAL PROPERTY,AN INVESTMENT

Making the right investments is key to improving the business value of your SME. Investing in equipment and materials, product development, marketing and research can dramatically improve your company's financial position by expanding its asset base and increasing its future productivity. The acquisition of intellectual property rights can have a similar effect. The markets will value your company on the basis of its assets, its ordinary business operations, as well as its prospects for profitability, which may be affected by the acquisition of decisive patents. Examples abound of SMEs whose commercial value has increased overnight following the acquisition of important patents attached to cutting-edge techniques.

Likewise, a good brand, with a solid reputation among consumers, will also increase the current value of your company and definitely contribute to making its products and services more attractive to consumers. Investing in building a good intellectual property portfolio is therefore much more than a defense against potential competitors. It is a way to increase the business value of your company and improve its future profitability.

LAT VALUE OF INTELLECTUAL PROPERTY ASSETS

Crucially, the legal protection of intellectual property makes intangibles exclusive property rights, albeit for a limited period. It allows your SME to claim ownership of its intangible assets and to exploit them to the maximum of their potential. In short, intellectual property protection makes intangibles "a little more tangible" by turning them into valuable proprietary assets that often can be sold in the marketplace.

If the innovative ideas, creative designs and influential brand images of your SME are not protected by intellectual property rights, any other company can freely and legally use them without limit. On the other hand, if they are protected by these rights, they acquire a concrete value for your company by becoming property rights which cannot be marketed or used without your authorization.

Investors, stock brokers and financial advisors, increasingly realizing this reality, have begun to value intellectual property assets at high value. Companies around the world, increasingly aware of the value of their intellectual property assets, have, in some cases, incorporated them into their balance sheets. Many of them, including SMEs, have begun to commit to periodically monitoring the management of their techniques and intellectual property. In many cases, companies have realized that their intellectual property assets are actually worth more than their tangible assets. This is often the case for companies operating in high-tech and knowledge-intensive sectors, or those with a well-known brand image.

VSCONTROL OF MANAGEMENT OF YOUR INTELLECTUAL PROPERTY

One way for your SME to be better able to exploit the potential benefits of its intellectual property assets and to extract their full value is to control intellectual property management. It would be better to entrust this task to external auditors, but often a preliminary check can be carried out within your company. This involves identifying, analyzing and evaluating your SME's intellectual property assets to ensure that you are using them to best advantage. By doing so, your SME will be able to make informed decisions in the following cases:

Acquisition of intellectual property assets– Knowing your company's intellectual property and its value will help you decide what kind of intellectual property rights to acquire and maintain and how best to administer your SME's intellectual property assets (see "Can your SME obtain and maintain intellectual property protection?" and "How to manage your SME's intellectual property assets").

Mergers and Acquisitions– A good knowledge of the intellectual property assets of your SME can significantly enhance it. Indeed, investors judge a company according to its forecasts of profitability, which are based, to a large extent, on the exploitation of intellectual property rights.

Grant of License– Your SME can increase its cash flow (revenue) by licensing its IP rights to a third party (see "How to license IP rights? An essential part of your SME's business strategy"). An intellectual property management audit will allow your SME to determine the value of your own intellectual property in order to obtain the maximum benefits from licensing agreements. The resulting revenue can increase the business value of your SME.

Pledge– A well-built intellectual property portfolio can also serve as collateral. In this case, the lessors will determine on the basis of the intellectual property assets the solvency position of your SME (see “Can your SME use intellectual property assets for financing purposes?”).

Enforcement of rights– Knowing the value of your intellectual property assets, your SME will be able to decide whether and how to sue for infringement in each case.

Cost reduction– A well-managed IP registry will help you, among other things, to discover obsolete IP assets (and thereby eliminate costs of maintaining these assets), to not infringe the IP rights of third parties, which , unquestionably, will reduce costs.

By becoming accustomed to inventorying and exploiting intellectual property assets and using them strategically, a company can increase its revenues, outperform its competitors and position itself well in the market; these are all strategies that can lead to a commercial revaluation of your SME.

SHOW TO TURN INVENTIONS INTO PROFITABLE ASSETS FOR YOUR SME?

Innovative and creative ideas are at the center of most money-making businesses. Ideas themselves, however, are of little value. They must be exploited, materialized into innovative products or services and their marketing ensured so that your SME can reap the fruits of its spirit of innovation and creativity. Intellectual property, especially patents, can be instrumental in transforming innovative ideas and inventions into competitive products that significantly increase profit margins.

Your SME can also receive royalties through the patent system by licensing its patented inventions to other companies that have the capacity to commercialize them. Thus, your SME, not only will save money, but it will also ensure an influx of revenue from its invention or the inventions of its employees, without having to invest to market them.

For practical information on patent costs, patent filing times and other frequently asked questions, you can consult the links or contact your national intellectual property office.

LREASONS TO PATENT YOUR INVENTIONS

Exclusive rights– Patents provide the exclusive rights that normally allow your SME to use and exploit the invention for twenty years from the date of filing the patent application.

Strong position in the market– Thanks to these exclusive rights, you can prevent third parties from using your patented invention commercially, thus reducing competition and exercising market supremacy.

Superior investment returns– Having invested considerable sums and time to develop innovative products, your SME can, under cover of these exclusive rights, commercialize the invention and thereby obtain a higher return on its investment.

Ability to license or sell the invention– If you prefer not to exploit the patent yourself, you can sell it or license the rights to commercialize it to another company that will generate revenue for you.

Increased bargaining power– If your SME takes care of acquiring the rights to use patents belonging to another company, through a licensing agreement, your patent portfolio will increase your bargaining power. In other words, the company you are negotiating with will have the greatest interest in your patents and you could enter into cross-licences which would, in essence, allow the two companies to exchange the rights attached to the patents.

Notoriety for your business– Business partners, investors and shareholders will see patent portfolios as evidence of the high level of competence, specialization and technical capability within your company. This will prove useful in raising funds, finding business partners and enhancing the business value of your company.

The documents "Formulating an Intellectual Property Development Strategy for Enterprises" (available in Adobe PDF format) and "The Role of IPRs in the Promotion of Competitiveness and Development of Enterprises" (available in Adobe PDF format) offer some insights on how to develop a patent strategy for your SME.

In many cases, where a company has simply improved an existing product and where the improvements are not inventive enough to be patentable, utility models (or "petty patents" or "utility certificates") will, where appropriate, provide in the country in question, a satisfactory variant. Sometimes it would be wise for your SME to keep its innovations in the form of trade secrets, which in particular obliges you to take the necessary measures to ensure confidentiality.

It is strongly recommended that SMEs involved in inventive activities consult patent databases to find out about existing techniques, seek licensing partners in the event that a technique already exists and avoid any duplication of research activities. There is a more detailed analysis of the importance of patent searches.

QU'HAPPENS-IT IF YOU DON'T PATENT YOUR INVENTIONS?

Someone else can patent them– In most countries (except the United States of America), the first person or company to file a patent application for an invention will be entitled to the patent. In fact, this means that if you do not patent your inventions or the inventions of your SME's employees, a third party - who subsequently develops an identical or equivalent invention - can do so and legitimately exclude your company from the market, limit its activities to the continuation of the previous employment when the patent legislation provides for an exception of this type, or ask your SME to pay a fee for use of the invention.

Competitors can profit from your invention– If the product is successful, many competing companies will be tempted to manufacture the same product using your invention without having to pay for its use. Large companies will take advantage of economies of scale to manufacture the product at a lower cost and impose a more favorable market price. These processes will significantly reduce your company's market share for this product. Small competing companies can also manufacture the same product and sell it cheaper, without having to offset the research and development costs incurred by your SME.

Possibilities to license, sell or transfer technology will be severely hampered– Without intellectual property rights, technology transfers will be difficult, if not impossible. To transfer a technique, it is necessary to have ownership of it, which only the protection of intellectual property can obtain. Moreover, during negotiations with a view to transferring a given technical innovation without it being protected by intellectual property rights, each party is wary of disclosing its invention, fearing that the other will walk away with it. Intellectual property protection, particularly patent protection, is essential for acquiring technology through licensing.

HASOTHER LINKS AND BIBLIOGRAPHIES

For additional information on how patents help SMEs to exploit their innovation potential, you can consult the following documents:

Formulating an Intellectual Property Development Strategy for Enterprises" (see WIPO/IP/HAN/98/7(b) in Adobe PDF format).

Fostering the Globalization Potential of SMEs in the Globalization Era

The Role of the IPR in the Promotion of Competitiveness and Development of Enterprises"

For a basic overview of patents and patentable inventions, see: "The Protection of Inventions: Patents and Other Titles of Protection" (see WIPO/IP/ADD/97/2 in Adobe PDF format).

WHY IS INTELLECTUAL PROPERTY ESSENTIAL TO THE MARKETING OF YOUR SME'S PRODUCTS OR SERVICES?

For most small and medium-sized enterprises (SMEs), marketing products or services is a major difficulty. A marketing strategy would make it possible to establish a clear link between your products or services and your SME as a producer or supplier of these products or services. This means that consumers could distinguish your products or services from those of your competitors at a glance and associate them with certain desired qualities.

Intellectual property, when used effectively, plays an important role in creating the image of your business in the minds of current and potential consumers and in positioning your business in the marketplace. Intellectual property rights, associated with other marketing tools (such as advertisements and other sales promotion activities) are essential for:

differentiate your products and services and make them more easily recognizable

promote your products or services and create a loyal customer base

diversify your marketing strategy to reach diverse consumer groups

market your products or services in foreign countries (see "Can intellectual property increase your SME's export possibilities?")

DINTELLECTUAL PROPERTY RIGHTS AND MARKETING

Different intellectual property rights can play a role in your go-to-market strategy in several ways:

Trademarks of products and services

A well-designed brand is often a decisive instrument for the success of your SME in the market. It will allow consumers to distinguish your SME's products or services from those of your competitors and to associate them with the desired qualities. Additionally, it can play an important role in your product or service's ability to break into a new market, especially if you have chosen or created the brand carefully to appeal to the intended audience. It is essential that you research any trademarks that may conflict with your own before applying for or using a new trademark for your goods or services. For this purpose, you can use the services of a lawyer or a competent agent.

Collective marks

The use of a collective mark (by a cooperative or an association of enterprises) allows SME members to take advantage of a reputation acquired on the basis of the common origin or other common characteristics of the goods produced or services provided by different companies. This is particularly the case when the origin or other common characteristics constitute the main factor of determination of the quality or good taste of a product or service. The use of a collective mark can promote an alliance or facilitate cooperation with other SMEs so as to take full advantage of common resources.

Industrial designs

In today's highly competitive global economy, a visually appealing design alone can help you attract a demanding and extremely diverse clientele. Through creative designs, your SME will be able to reach and attract diverse groups of consumers from different age groups, regions, cultures etc. different. Owning the design rights to the attractive shape or style of a product can give you a very useful advantage over competitors.

Geographical indications

Consumers of certain products from a given region expect to find certain characteristics inherent in these products that derive from the soil, climate or the particular know-how of the inhabitants of this region. Exploiting the reputation of your products that come from such a region or leveraging such skills in your marketing strategy is a good business tactic to differentiate your products from those of others. It is important to emphasize that with such products, your SME must maintain the standards and quality expected of products from that region or such know-how. See "Geographical Indications".

Patents

The product that you have recently introduced to a market may indeed qualify for patent protection. Having a patent can also open up other business avenues such as licensing or entering into strategic alliances (see “How to turn inventions into profitable assets for your SME?”).

Utility models

Effective use of utility models or certificates, where such protection is possible, can help your SME keep up with its competitors. When used strategically, utility model protection can be an effective instrument to position your SME in the market, especially if it operates in an area where technological advantage plays an important role in determining which company has the largest market share. By taking a close look at your competitors' products and the profit promises they represent, you can always improve your SME's products to deliver the same or better benefits and protect your innovation as a utility model.

LA MARKETING YOUR PRODUCTS AND SERVICES IN THE NEW ECONOMY

The impact of e-commerce on intellectual property and your SME

While the Internet can provide many opportunities for SMEs, it can also pose a number of obstacles to the effective protection and enforcement of intellectual property rights generally and copyright and related rights, trademarks and patents in particular. Protection under copyright and related rights in the digital environment, the possibility of patent protection for e-commerce business methods, the use of trademarks such as "metatags" and keywords, infringements of rights attached to trademarks through the use of a sign on the Internet, the scope of protection for well-known trademarks and unfair competition in electronic commerce are the main controversial questions and challenges that your SME will have to solve or to relieve. For more information, see "Intellectual Property and Electronic Commerce".

Domain names

If you plan to do business on the Internet you need an Internet address, technically called a domain name. Although having a different function, domain names often conflict with trademarks which are used to identify your products and services and distinguish them from those of your competitors. Your SME should therefore avoid using a domain name already protected by another company as a trademark. If your SME is faced with the use of its trademark as a domain name by a competitor, you can seek advice on how to resolve a dispute effectively and at a reasonable cost. While many disputes between trademarks and domain names can be settled by the courts, many SMEs may prefer to have recourse to faster and cheaper special procedures within the framework of alternative dispute resolution mechanisms. WIPO's Domain Name Dispute Resolution Service is the leading institution in this area.

Others I here you documents

TMAKE THE MOST OF INTELLECTUAL PROPERTY PROTECTION

In order to ensure that your marketing program makes the most of your intellectual property rights, it is useful to consider the following acts:

Register your intellectual property assets or seek their protection as soon as possible in order to take full advantage of your intellectual property rights while engaging in advertising and other promotional activities.

Carefully check that your SME does not infringe the intellectual property rights of third parties. In this regard, it is advisable to carry out research on trademarks and patents before marketing products and services that may conflict with intellectual property rights protected by other persons or companies.

Use or refer to your intellectual property rights in your advertisements or other promotional activities to inform your current and potential customers about the protection of your products and services by intellectual property.

Monitor the market and be prepared to contact an IP lawyer or official IP enforcement body when you become aware of any infringement of your IP rights that may affect profits or your SME's reputation (see “How can your SME resolve intellectual property disputes?”). In practice, intellectual property rights allow you to fight against unauthorized reproduction, imitation and other types of infringement. National law or case law may also provide protection against acts of unfair competition such as false claims intended to discredit your products or services,

CAN YOUR SME USE INTELLECTUAL PROPERTY ASSETS FOR FINANCING PURPOSES?

There has been a growing realization in recent years that intellectual property assets can be monetized. There are several ways to do this. Intellectual property can be sold, licensed, used as collateral or collateral for credit, or, additionally or in parallel, as security for borrowing funds from friends, family, private investors (known as in English "business angels" who invest in small and medium-sized companies not listed on the stock exchange and often offer their experience and expertise), venture capitalists, specialized banks and sometimes even ordinary banks.

In addition, in most countries, the government encourages and supports new technology companies and other innovative SMEs through grants, guarantees, grants, possibly concessional loans, which are provided through public credit and banks that realize directly or indirectly the importance of intellectual property assets.

As the owner or manager of an SME, it is therefore important that you consider your company's intellectual property not only as a legal asset but also as a financial instrument.

QPRACTICAL INTELLECTUAL PROPERTY ISSUES WHEN'ELABORATION OF'A DEVELOPMENT PLAN

What can a development plan do for you?

A business plan is a mechanism to ensure that a company's resources or assets are usefully employed in all activities in order to gain and maintain a competitive advantage in the market. For a new business it is a blueprint for success and for an existing business the plan provides an overview of where the business is, how it positions itself and seeks to achieve its goals for become or remain a successful business.

Developing a development plan takes a lot of work. So what justifies the time and energy you are going to put into developing a plan? A development plan can be used for several purposes:

Investigate the possibility of realizing your business idea: an established business plan obliges a company to consider all the essential questions, namely the potential demand for its products or services, the nature of the competition, the barriers to entry, the axis of the specific commercial proposal of the new or improved products or services, the resources required, the necessary number of employees, the appropriate technologies and strategic partners, the search for financing, the expected start-up costs, the marketing strategies and others.

Get access to services and start-up funds: Business incubators and potential investors and funders require well-designed and realistic business plans. Since this is often not the case, it is no wonder that investors and business incubators reject 80% of the business plans they receive.

Provide strategic direction: A development plan is a reference document that provides your management team and yourself with an objective basis to determine if your business is on track to achieve its goals within the set time frame and with the available resources.

Provide a standard or benchmark for evaluating business decisions and outcomes in the future. This standard or benchmark may evolve with the business and the development plan is, as such, a living document that needs to be revised based on new and changing circumstances.

Why should intellectual property be part of your development plan?

New or original knowledge and the creative expression of ideas is a driving force behind successful 21st century businesses. Therefore, the protection of such knowledge and creative expressions from inadvertent disclosure or unauthorized use by competitors plays an increasingly critical role in gaining and maintaining competitive advantage. Starting a business also requires various other types of resources, including a network of contacts and funds. The intellectual property protection system is a key instrument to 1) ward off unscrupulous competitors, 2) strengthen relationships with employees, consultants, suppliers, contractors, business partners and customers, and
3) obtain funds.

To be accepted by a business incubator or to attract investors, it is necessary to have a quality development plan that objectively presents the prospects of the proposed business. To convince investors, you must demonstrate 1) that there is a demand for your product in the market, 2) that your product is better than competing products, if any, and 3) that you have taken the adequate measures to prevent your success from being "parasitized" by dishonest competitors.

Most entrepreneurs would claim that the product they offer is innovative, unique, or superior to competitors' offerings. But is this really the case? If you think so, you have to prove it, and a patent (or the results of a reliable patent search) may be your best proof of novelty.

Trade names, trademarks and domain names can be the essential elements in distinguishing your product from those of competitors. Therefore, the trade name, trademark(s) and domain name(s) you offer should be chosen carefully and the steps taken to register them should be mentioned in your business plan.

En outre, les prestataires de services aux nouvelles entreprises de haute technologie et les investisseurs voudront s'assurer que le produit que vous proposez de vendre ne se fonde pas indûment sur les secrets d'affaire, les contenus protégés, les brevets ou d'autres droits de propriété intellectuelle appartenant à d'autres entreprises, ce qui pourrait causer la chute de votre propre entreprise à la suite de procès coûteux. Dans certains secteurs de pointe, le risque d'atteinte aux droits de propriété intellectuelle d'un tiers est élevé et les prestataires de services aux nouvelles entreprises de haute technologie et les investisseurs peuvent être réticents à s'engager si vous ne prouvez pas l'absence de risque (par exemple au moyen d'une recherche en matière de brevets ou de marques).

For many companies, confidential business information (such as production information, secret inventions, as well as technical, financial and marketing know-how) can alone create an advantage.

competitive. Under such conditions, it is important to inform tech start-up service providers and investors that your company has important trade secrets (known as trade secrets) and that you have taken adequate steps to protect them. employees and competitors. In fact, even the development plan itself is a secret document to which access should be selective and, generally speaking, permitted only after the employee has signed a non-disclosure or confidentiality agreement. , the investor or any other relevant person.

In short, if intellectual property is an important asset for your business (i.e. if you own patents or patentable techniques, industrial designs, trade secrets, recognized trademarks or if you you hold economic rights to protected works), it must represent an essential aspect of your development plan. The proper disclosure of a company's assets and market opportunities should not only list tangible assets (e.g. plants, equipment, capital, etc.) but also intangible assets since the latter constitute more moreover the key to the success of companies in an extremely competitive environment. As such,

How can intellectual property be integrated into the development plan development process?

Writing a plan requires good preparation. You must first consider a number of questions. You need to know the nature of your business, know what resources are needed to achieve the objectives, identify your target markets, assess the solidity and the possibilities of growth of the business etc. Additionally, you should determine the commercial utility of intellectual property assets, whether owned by you or licensed by another company, and the resources required to acquire and maintain those assets.

The discussion below lists some key questions about IP aspects that you need to consider when developing your business plan. The different points will be more or less important depending on your particular situation and your activities. Moreover, this list is not exhaustive, many other aspects must be taken into consideration according to your particularities. However, the answers to these questions can help you integrate IP assets into the process of developing your business plan.

1. What intellectual property assets do you hold?

Define and categorize your intellectual property portfolio. This always contains confidential information or business secrets, one or more trade names and one or more trademarks, it also often contains domain names, industrial designs or models, titles of copyright and rights related products, and sometimes utility models and patents.

What other intangible assets do you have? In this regard, also consider franchise, licensing and distribution agreements, publishing rights, non-competition clauses, information databases, software information technology, business profile, management knowledge, distribution network, technical skills, etc.

2. What is the status of your intellectual property portfolio?

Do you have a system for determining your intellectual property assets?

Do you hold an intellectual property portfolio? When was it created? By who?

Which of your intellectual property assets are subject to registration? Are they registered or should they be? Are they also registered in foreign countries or in export markets? Does the registration need to be renewed? If yes, when?

Do you carry out management checks of your intellectual property or do you plan to do so? If so, how often and who is responsible for it?

3. How do you plan to protect your intellectual property assets?

If you commercialize your intellectual property assets (whether individually or with a partner), do you benefit from arrangements that guarantee ownership or co-ownership?

If you subcontract part of your commercial activities, have you established contracts guaranteeing your intellectual property rights on the subcontracted work and prohibiting third parties from profiting from your products or marketing them without your prior agreement?

How easy or difficult is it for others to obtain or properly reproduce your secret business information? What steps are taken to ensure the secrecy of your confidential business information?
Do you have an integrated security policy and plan for your physical and electronic assets? If you market your intellectual property assets (whether personally or with a partner), do you have arrangements in place to ensure the confidentiality of your secret business information?
Have you introduced confidentiality or non-disclosure clauses and non-competition clauses in the employment contracts of your key employees and agreements with your business partners?

Have you ensured that confidential business information or trade secrets are not made available or disclosed by posting on or through your website? Are all your URL headers free of confidential information? Do your web pages contain links to pages hosting confidential information?

4. What is the role of IP assets in the success of your business?

To what extent are your IP assets actually used or potentially useful, or no longer used by your business?

Does the commercial success of your business depend on intellectual property assets, whether owned or licensed by your business? What types of intellectual property assets are these?

Do you have new products or processes that will give you a unique competitive advantage? If so, will they revolutionize an industrial sector? Can the related intellectual property rights be secured to provide additional differentiation and prevent competitors from entering the market?

What competitive advantage do your intellectual property assets (owned or licensed) give your business? Evaluate and explain the extent to which the intellectual property provides customer interest and contributes to the acquisition of a sustainable competitive advantage.

Are your trade secrets, patents, trademarks, copyrighted works and industrial designs enough to protect the elements of your business that determine its success?

5. Do you own all the IP assets you need or are you dependent on IP assets held by third parties?

Do you own the intellectual property assets you use? Can you prove it? Do you have records, records, contracts, and other evidence that an investor, business partner, or court may require? Have you identified complaints that third parties may file regarding your intellectual property titles (for example, industrial sponsors or beneficiaries of research contracts)?

Are you sure you are not infringing the intellectual property rights of a third party? Can you prove it (eg have you done a patent, trademark or industrial design search)? Have you verified that none of your key employees who have worked for a competitor in the past are bound by non-competition or confidentiality and non-competition agreements? post-employment non-disclosure with a previous employer? Do you need access to third party intellectual property to exploit your business idea? Have you been granted the licenses you need to use the intellectual property that you do not own?

Have you signed non-disclosure or non-competition agreements with key members of your staff, contractors, consultants or other outside vendors who transfer to your company any intellectual property they create when do they work for you?

When you use outside vendors to write and design your marketing or advertising materials or your website and web pages, do the contracts specify who owns the intellectual property created as part of this? If employees initiate a creation, is it within the scope of their duties? If not, have you provided a written deed of assignment of the copyright and other intellectual property rights concerned? Do you have proper permissions to use, on your website or any other manner, written documents, drawings, photographs, music or anything else, created by a third party?

- Does your website contain meta tags, hyperlinks, frames or other strong links to other websites? Have the third parties concerned duly given their authorization for this?

6. Do you have sufficient knowledge of your competitors' IP strategies and IP portfolios?

Do you have a plan for gathering competitive information? Do you collect IP information and databases or plan to use them to gain insights to be more competitive than your competitors? By searching patent, trademark, and industrial design registers, you can obtain detailed legal, technical, and business information about a competitor's operations and products. You can use this information to estimate if there might be a market for your products. In addition, an intellectual property search allows you to check whether you can protect your intellectual property,

Are there any intellectual property barriers preventing you from entering your competitor's market, such as patents, trademarks or industrial designs, highlighting consumer loyalty to the competitor's image and brands, etc.?

7. Do you have an intellectual property policy and strategy in place for your company?

How do you generally identify, protect, exploit and manage your intellectual property assets?

What projects have you put in place to derive the maximum benefit from the commercialization of your intellectual property assets?

Do you have a particular marketing strategy? Do you plan to export? If yes, do you use or do you plan to use a regional or international filing or registration system (such as the Patent Cooperation Treaty, Madrid System or Hague Agreement) for applications patent and trademark or design registrations?

Have you evaluated the possibilities of commercializing all or part of your intellectual property assets wholly or partially through licensing, franchising or sales?

Have you submitted your intellectual property to independent management review on a regular basis? Have your intellectual property assets been valued? Was it done independently?

To what extent have you considered tax issues and incentives associated with commercializing your intellectual property? This operation may be subject to prior tax conditions (eg registration). The taxation regime for income and expenses arising from the commercialization of your intellectual property may deviate significantly from the accounting system. Government financial assistance measures can be applied to intellectual property assets and their commercialization.

Do you plan to use your intellectual property assets as collateral or security for a loan or to establish a tradable title in the securities market?
What are the possibilities for securitizing future revenue streams related to a group or portfolio of intellectual property assets owned by you?

Do you have a staff training program covering the management and protection of your intellectual property assets?

Business plans are an essential tool for engaging tech start-up service providers and investors and exploring opportunities for your business. Because intellectual property gives your business competitive advantages and increases its value, it is necessary to make your intellectual property assets known to new high-tech business service providers and investors by integrating them appropriately into your plan. of development.

USING INTELLECTUAL PROPERTY ASSETS TO FINANCE YOUR BUSINESS

Intellectual property assets can help support your request for funds from investors or lenders. The investor or lender, whether a bank, a financial institution, a venture capitalist or a private investor, will verify, to assess the request for assistance or loan financial, if the new or innovative product or service offered by the SME is protected by a patent, utility model, trademark, industrial design or model, copyright or related rights. Protection of this type is often a good indicator of the potential your SME has to succeed in the market.

The ownership of intellectual property rights is therefore an important element in convincing investors or lenders of the market possibilities available to the company to market the product or service in question. Sometimes a single dominating patent can open the doors to many financial opportunities.

Ownership of intellectual property rights over the creation or innovations attached to products or services that a company intends to market guarantees a certain degree of exclusivity and, consequently, a higher market share if the product or service has success with consumers.

Investors or lenders may value your intellectual property assets in different ways and attach different degrees of importance to intellectual property rights. However, there is a clear trend to bet more and more on intellectual property assets, which represent a competitive advantage for companies. Also, investors or lenders are increasingly turning to companies with a well-managed intellectual property portfolio, although they face, even in developed countries, many new problems and challenges.

As the owner or manager of an SME, you should therefore take steps to understand the commercial value of your company's intellectual property assets, ensuring that they are appraised by specialists, if necessary, as well as any instructions to duly declare them in detail in the accounting records and on the balance sheet. In particular, be sure to identify your SME's intellectual property assets in the business plan that you present to potential investors or lenders.

LE SURETY OF INTELLECTUAL PROPERTY ASSETS:A NEW TREND

Lending money fully or partially secured by intellectual property assets is a recent phenomenon even in developed countries. The pledging of commercial loans and bank credits with collateral represented by intellectual property assets is increasingly common, particularly in the music industry, Internet SMEs and high-tech sectors.

Suretyship generally means the pooling of different financial assets and the issuance of new securities guaranteed by these assets. In principle, these can be receivables that are based on reasonably reliable cash, or even exclusive receivables. It is thus possible to guarantee the payment of royalties resulting from the licensing of a patent, a trademark or a trade secret, or the rights of a musician attached to works or musical recordings. Thus, one of the most notorious guarantees of recent years concerned the payment of royalties from a rock specialist in the United States, namely
Mr David Bowie.

Currently, markets for securities backed by intellectual property assets are small, with few buyers and sellers. But given the recent proliferation of intellectual property exchanges on the Internet, it is likely that over time all interested parties will devote more attention and resources to the use of intellectual property assets to fund the new business creation and expansion. The more liquidity the intellectual property creates, the more opportunities there will be for collateral.

IIMPORTANCE D'A FAIR ASSESSMENT OF INTELLECTUAL PROPERTY TO OBTAIN FUNDING

While securitization seems to be gaining ground, traditional loans remain the main source of external financing for most SMEs. The practice of providing loans secured only by intellectual property assets is not very common; in fact this technique is used more by venture capital investment companies than by banks. If you want to use IP assets as collateral for financing, you are more likely to succeed if you can demonstrate that your IP assets have some liquidity and can be valued independently of your business. In addition, you must demonstrate that your intellectual property assets are durable, at least for the duration of your loan repayment,

In this regard, it is essential to identify all of your SME's intellectual property assets and obtain an objective valuation of them by a competent valuation company. The value of intellectual property management procedures that identify, record, analyze and encrypt your intellectual property assets is growing in the Internet marketplace. This is an additional reason for you to do better internal knowledge of the scope and value of intellectual property assets, including trade secrets, that could be used as collateral for a loan.

It is true that the valuation of intellectual property has until now been considered highly subjective by lenders and borrowers. Although there are well-established assessment methods, these are considered too subjective or generally misunderstood by most people. However, the increasing use of royalty streams from licensing to determine the value of intellectual property is a positive development that will strengthen the acceptance of intellectual property assets as valuable assets providing security for the debt financing and equity lending.

As an SME, it is therefore important that you keep this aspect in mind when looking for specific financial assistance and developing a business strategy and action program for your business.

HASOTHER LINKS AND DOCUMENTS

The European Business Angels Network promotes the exchange of experience between networks of private investors and has indirect impacts through a range of advisory and display functions, direct feedback from investors to SMEs and an educational role and training for all participants.

The European Venture Capital Association's website provides links to a large number of national venture capital associations around the world.

The website of the European Commission provides information and links to other sources of funding for innovative activities and their commercialization.

The "Innovation 2000" initiative of the European Investment Bank (EIB) marks a clear reorientation of lending activities in favor of projects with a high innovation content and is structured around five main components, one of which concerns "SMEs and the creation of companies". The support provided by the EIB mainly takes the form of loan operations and venture capital financing schemes for SMEs (through its specialized subsidiary, the European Investment Fund - EIF - As regards 'SMEs and business creation', the support is aimed at risk capital operations and guarantees for debt financing, which are managed by the EIF (see paragraph 7 of the first cited webpage).

The February 2001 study report on the financing of innovative companies by venture capital, while studying the situation in Europe, makes a comparison with the United States and also examines Israel; this report is available in English at

The National Venture Capital Association website provides an introduction to venture capital in the United States of America.

Article titled "Financing and Securing Intellectual Property" at

Article titled "IP Assets as Sources of Potential Corporate Profits" at

Article entitled "Venture Capital in Canada: Focus on Small and Medium Technology Enterprises" at

Article titled “Has David Bowie Started a New Era of Celebrity Securitizations?” at the address

Article titled “Financing E-Commerce: Legal and Practical Risks” at.

CAN INTELLECTUAL PROPERTY INCREASE YOUR SME'S EXPORT OPPORTUNITIES?

Before committing to an export operation, companies must go through a series of key steps: identifying a suitable export market, estimating demand, finding distribution channels, estimating costs and obtaining funds. Here we seek to highlight the main reasons why you should also consider intellectual property issues when planning your export strategy and consider how intellectual property rights could enhance the competitiveness of your small or medium-sized business. (SMEs) in export markets.

Since intellectual property rights are "territorial", i.e. you can only rely on them in the country or region for which they were requested and granted, to benefit from copyright proprietary intellectual property in foreign markets, you must seek and obtain protection abroad (unless it is possible to obtain the rights automatically without having to complete any formalities, for example through an international treaty mechanism such as the Berne Convention for the Protection of Literary and Artistic Works, see "How can your SME benefit from copyright protection?").

The main reasons for protecting intellectual property in export markets are set out below:

Intellectual property rights, especially patents, can open up new export opportunities.

Intellectual property rights, especially trademarks and industrial designs, can help you create a favorable position in export markets.

Intellectual property rights increase the chances of winning loyal customers for your products and services in export markets.

EEXPORT YOUR PATENTED PRODUCTS

Patent (or utility model) protection gives you a significant competitive advantage in export markets. Companies that have well protected their inventions abroad have a series of possibilities to export their innovative products, which otherwise might not be the case. Among these possibilities are the following:

Manufacture the product domestically and export the protected product, directly or through intermediarics, knowing that no other company can legally manufacture, sell or exploit the same product in the designated market without your authorization (and that most legislation patents no longer allow, in accordance with the country's international obligations, to issue non-voluntary licenses on the grounds that the protected products are not manufactured locally in the country of export destination).

Licensing the invention to a foreign company that will manufacture the product locally, in return for the payment of a lump sum and/or royalties (see "How to license intellectual property rights? An essential part of commercial strategy of your SME").

Create joint ventures with other companies for the manufacture and/or marketing of the product in selected foreign markets.

Depending on your strategy, your business will earn additional revenue either through the direct sale of the product or through taxes and/or royalties paid by a licensee.

UUSE L'BRAND IMAGE AND DESIGNS TO MARKET AL PRODUCTS AND SERVICES'FOREIGNER

The reasons for the protection of trademarks and industrial designs in the domestic market are also fully valid for foreign markets.
Trademark registration, in particular, allows you to maximize product differentiation, advertising and marketing, thereby enhancing recognition of your product or service in international markets and creating a direct link with foreign consumers. Depending on the nature of your service, a franchise agreement with companies abroad could be another attractive solution to also collect revenue from your brand abroad.

Companies that export unbranded products will face disadvantages such as:

lower incomes as consumers demand lower prices for unbranded products;

lack of consumer loyalty due in large part to their inability to recognize the product and distinguish it from those of competitors;

difficulties in marketing and advertising products and services abroad in the absence of an appropriate symbol or simple identifier linking your products or services to your SME, as marketing an unbranded product is inherently much more difficult.

As far as industrial designs are concerned, protection in export markets will not only help strengthen your overall business strategy, but it will also play an important role in adapting products to certain target markets, creating niche for your company's products and enhancing your company's image and reputation by linking to a particular design.

EINTERNATIONAL DRAWING AND PARALLEL IMPORT

When developing your export strategy, you should ascertain, preferably by consulting a competent specialist, whether a buyer can legally resell in another market products protected by intellectual property rights which he has purchased from your SME, or with your consent, without seeking your permission. This question will only arise if you have already secured protection for your intellectual property rights domestically as well as in export markets, or if you consider requesting it. Similarly, if your SME has purchased products protected by a patent, trademark, industrial design or model and/or copyright, you should check whether you need to obtain the formal agreement of the copyright holder. intellectual property to be able to sell these goods abroad, i.e. in other markets (i.e. to check whether the intellectual property rights are considered to be "exhausted"). You may be surprised by the fact that the answers to these questions are quite complex and may not only vary from country to country but also depend on the type of intellectual property right concerned.

Before examining these questions, it is necessary to define what is meant by the "exhaustion" of intellectual property rights. "Exhaustion" constitutes one of the limits of intellectual property rights. Once a product protected by an intellectual property right has been commercialized by your SME or by others with your consent, the intellectual property rights to the commercial exploitation of this product can no longer be exercised by your SME because they are "exhausted". This limitation is sometimes also referred to as the "first sale theory" because the rights to commercially exploit a given product expire with the first sale of that product. Unless otherwise provided by law, subsequent acts of resale, rental, lending or other forms of commercial use by third parties can no longer be controlled or challenged by your SME. There is a relatively broad consensus in favor of the application of this principle at least within the framework of the national market.

There is less consensus on the question of whether the sale abroad of a product protected by intellectual property rights can exhaust the intellectual property rights in that product under national law. The question becomes relevant in the so-called "parallel importation" cases. This practice consists of importing products outside the distribution channels contractually negotiated with the manufacturer. Since the manufacturer/owner of the intellectual property right has no contractual relationship with the parallel importer, the imported products are sometimes referred to as "grey market products", which is often misleading in practice because the products are originals , but the distribution channels are not controlled by the manufacturer/owner of the intellectual property right. On the basis of the right to import conferred by an intellectual property right on its holder, the latter may attempt to oppose such importation in order to separate the markets. However, if the marketing of the product abroad by the owner of the intellectual property right or with his consent leads to the exhaustion of the right at the national level, the import right is also exhausted and can therefore no longer be invoked against parallel import.

The above principles have different implications depending on whether the importing country, for legislative or political reasons, applies the principle of national, regional or international exhaustion. The principle of national exhaustion does not authorize the holder of the intellectual property right to control the commercial exploitation of the products put by him, or with his consent, on the national market. However, the holder of the intellectual property right (or the licensee to whom he has given authorisation) can always oppose the importation of original products marketed abroad, on the basis of the import right. In case of regional exhaustion, the first sale by the right holder or with his consent of the product protected by an intellectual property right constitutes the exhaustion of all intellectual property rights on these products, not only at the national level but throughout the region, and parallel imports into the region can no longer be objected to on the basis of intellectual property rights. When a country applies the principle of international exhaustion, intellectual property rights are exhausted as soon as the product has been sold by the right holder or with his consent in any region of the world. and parallel imports into the region can no longer be objected to on the basis of intellectual property rights. When a country applies the principle of international exhaustion, intellectual property rights are exhausted as soon as the product has been sold by the right holder or with his consent in any region of the world. and parallel imports into the region can no longer be objected to on the basis of intellectual property rights. When a country applies the principle of international exhaustion, intellectual property rights are exhausted as soon as the product has been sold by the right holder or with his consent in any region of the world.

National intellectual property offices, or intellectual property lawyers or agents, should be able to inform you of the provisions or specific cases that apply in the country concerned for each type of intellectual property right.

For more information on recent decisions and different approaches in civil law and common law countries and internationally, see document ATRIP/GVA/99/6 entitled "Parallel Imports and International Trade" (available in Adobe format PDF) (presented at the Annual Meeting of the International Association for the Advancement of Teaching and Research in Intellectual Property (ATRIP) held at WIPO Headquarters in Geneva (from 7 to 9 July 1999).

HASOTHER LINKS AND DOCUMENTS

You can find advice on exporting your products on the following websites:

international trade center.
This website contains a register of trade promotion agencies and other trade support institutions.

Tradenet Export Advisors. This website provides guidance on various aspects of exporting. Although some questions are discussed from the perspective of US exporters, the explanations are often general and helpful.
to SMEs in all countries. See in particular the part entitled "Export answers" .

World Chambers Network. This website provides trade and business information by country and contains a register of chambers of commerce around the world.

Organization of American States.This website contains information by country for exporters doing business with countries in Latin America or North America, in the SICE database under the heading "Trade and Integration".

BizAPEC is a business service provided by the APEC Secretariat. This site contains information on business and investment in Asia-Pacific Economic Cooperation countries.

SBA's Guide to exportingis aimed in particular at American companies .

CAN YOUR SME OBTAIN AND MAINTAIN INTELLECTUAL PROPERTY PROTECTION?

Before you can profit from intellectual property assets, your SME must acquire intellectual property rights. A number of rights must be granted or registered. At the national level, the intellectual property offices of the various countries are the only institutions empowered to grant or register intellectual property rights. The procedure for obtaining and maintaining may vary from country to country, but the principles and fundamental characteristics of these procedures are the same in most countries. It should be noted that intellectual property rights can also, under certain conditions, be obtained at regional or international level (see "Protecting your SME's intellectual property rights abroad").

Before seeking intellectual property protection for your SME in a country, it is in your best interest to study the legal system that governs intellectual property issues. There are various sources of information on intellectual property legislation. To start, it would probably be best to contact the national intellectual property office or copyright office to obtain precise information on the protection of intellectual property in your country. In addition, you can consult WIPO's collection of laws accessible online (CLEA). It is often helpful to seek the assistance of an intellectual property agent or attorney, in particular where relevant intellectual property laws require an applicant not resident in the country to be represented by an agent or attorney licensed to practice in that country. The IP office, or IP agent/lawyer should be able to tell you if SMEs can benefit from special incentives, in the form of reduced fees, for obtaining and maintaining intellectual property rights.

Procedures for different intellectual property rights

The procedure for obtaining protection and maintaining intellectual property rights by your SME is described below:

BCOATINGS

The patent confers an exclusive right on an invention, which is a product or a process offering a new manner of making something or bringing a new technical solution to a problem.

Some general indications on the procedures for granting and maintaining patents

In a number of countries, patents are granted when the main patentability criteria (novelty, inventive step and industrial applicability) are deemed to be satisfied. However, many countries do not conduct substantive reviews due to financial or other constraints. These offices simply carry out an examination of the formalities that you must complete before filing your patent application. Among the countries that carry out a substantive examination, some do so automatically upon receipt of a patent application, while others do so only upon filing of a request to that effect. This request for examination must be filed within a certain period which, according to the legislation applicable to patents, can be up to several years. According to it is possible to postpone the examination and file an opposition before the granting of the patent, the procedure for granting a patent can be very long. Efforts are therefore being made, in many countries and at the international level, to speed up the procedure prior to the grant of the patent. In addition, a number of countries provide for the publication of patent applications after a certain period of time (generally 18 months after the date of filing or, where priority is claimed, after the priority date (see Frequently Asked Questions)).

The applicant must generally pay a filing fee and sometimes an examination fee (when a substantive examination is carried out) and an annual maintenance fee for the application. In most countries, patent maintenance fees must be paid each year (annuities). In accordance with international obligations under the Paris Convention for the Protection of Industrial Property and the Agreement on Trade-Related Aspects of Intellectual Property Rights (TRIPS Agreement), there is a minimum grace period of six months for failure to pay maintenance fees, but countries are free to grant longer grace periods. Failure to pay the maintenance fees within the grace period will result in the retroactive forfeiture of the patent,

For all practical information on the costs of issuing a patent, the time required to issue patents and any other useful FAQ, consult the links or contact your national intellectual property office.

MODELES D'USEFULNESS

In some countries, inventions may also be protected by utility models, which are also known as "petty patents" or "utility certificates". The conditions for registering utility models are generally less stringent (since no inventive step is required, or only less inventive step), the registration procedure is faster (since novelty and invention are generally subject to examination before registration) and the fees for obtaining and maintaining in force are generally lower than those applicable to patents.
Applications must generally be filed with the national intellectual property office.

MPRODUCT AND SERVICE BRANDS

A product or service mark is a distinctive sign that indicates that goods or services are produced or supplied by a certain person, business or group of people/businesses, enabling consumers to distinguish them from goods or third-party services.

Some general indications on trademark registration procedures

In some countries, trademark protection can be obtained by registration or use. In other countries, for most marks, you must register them if you wish to obtain their protection. Even when you can benefit from protection without registration, ie based on the use of the mark, it is always desirable to register the mark to obtain better or stronger protection.

If you wish to obtain protection for your SME's trademark by registration, you must file an application with a regional trademark office, if there is one, or a national one. As soon as the fees due have been paid, the office will examine the application. A number of reasons may lead to your application being rejected. In practice, requests are most often rejected for the following reasons:

i) it is likely that consumers will confuse your mark with a mark already on the register or for which an application has been filed or with an unregistered well-known mark;

ii) your mark only describes a product or service or a feature of the product or service;

iii) your brand is made up of a geographic term that may be confusing or should not be the monopoly of one company;

iv) your trademark violates public order or morality;

v) or your mark consists of an element, or contains it without authorization, which is identical to an official sign, coat of arms, flag or other protected emblem, or the hallmark of a State or an intergovernmental organization or in constitutes an imitation.

When the trademark law of a country provides for an opposition procedure, the application is published after it has been examined and after any interested person has had the opportunity to object to the registration of the mark if he considers that this could infringe his rights. The office will then render a decision based on the evidence provided by both parties and this decision will usually be appealed.

According to national laws, the initial registration period is at least seven years (usually 10 years). However, unlike other industrial property rights, trademark registration can be renewed indefinitely upon payment of a renewal fee. See also "Performing a trademark search".

MCOLLECTIVE ARCHS

Although the definition may vary from country to country, collective marks are generally defined as signs which characterize the geographical origin, the material used, the method of manufacture, the quality or other characteristics common to the products. or services of different companies using the collective mark. The owner can be an association of which these companies are members or any other entity, including a public institution or a cooperative. Most countries require that an application for a collective mark be accompanied by a copy of the regulations governing the use of the collective mark and do not allow the licensing of such a mark. Like product/service marks,

MNOTORIOUS ARCHS

Well-known trademarks and service marks enjoy protection in most countries against signs which arc considered to constitute a reproduction, imitation or translation of the mark, provided that they are likely to create confusion in the minds of the relevant sector of the public. Well-known marks are generally protected, regardless of whether they are registered or not, against goods and services identical or similar to those for which they have acquired their reputation. In many countries they are also, under certain conditions, protected against products and services that are not similar. It should be noted that, while there is no commonly agreed precise definition of what constitutes a "

Protection of well-known marks

Many countries protect unregistered well-known marks in accordance with their international obligations under the Paris Convention for the Protection of Industrial Property and the Agreement on Trade-Related Aspects of Intellectual Property Rights (Agreement on TRIPS). Therefore, no only large companies but also SMEs can stand a good chance of building sufficient reputation with consumers that their marks can be recognized as well-known marks and obtain protection without registration. However, it is advisable to apply for registration, given that many countries offer extended protection to registered well-known marks against impairment (Article 16.3 of the TRIPS Agreement), i.e. against the fact that the reputation of a mark is weakened by the unauthorized use of this mark by third parties.

You should be aware that a number of trademark laws simply implement the obligations under Article 16.3 of the TRIPS Agreement and only protect registered well-known marks under the following conditions:

the goods and services for which the other mark is used or for which protection is sought are not identical or similar to the goods for which the well-known mark has acquired its reputation,

the use of the other mark would indicate a link between these products and the owner o f the notorious mark

and could harm the latter's interests.

IINDICATIONSG E O G R A P H I C A L

What is a geographical indication?

A geographical indication is a sign used on products which have a precise geographical origin and which possess qualities or a notoriety due to this place of origin. Most of the time, a geographical indication consists of the name of the place of origin of the products. Agricultural products generally have qualities that derive from where they are produced and are influenced by specific local factors, such as climate and soil. For a sign to function as a geographical indication, national legislation must contain provisions to that effect and consumers must consider it as such. Geographical indications can be used for a wide variety of agricultural products; for example, the term "Tuscany" is used for the oil of

DDRAWINGS AND INDUSTRIAL MODELS

Industrial designs are line or color compositions or three-dimensional shapes that give a particular appearance to the industrial or handicraft product. They protect the ornamental or aesthetic aspect of a useful object, which generally appeals to the senses of sight or touch, and can be reproduced in large quantities.

Some general indications on industrial design protection procedures

In most countries, industrial design protection can only be obtained by registration. In a number of these countries, no search is carried out and no substantive examination is carried out before the industrial design is registered. Some countries provide for search and examination when the industrial design application has been published and a third party has objected to the registration in filing a notice of objection. In a very small number of countries, protection is also possible for unregistered industrial designs.

As a general rule, in order to qualify for protection by registration, the design must be "new" or "original". The term of protection varies from country to country.
While the usual term of protection is 15 years (an initial term of five years with the possibility of renewal for two additional periods of five years each), some countries offer protection for only 10 years while others go up to 25 years old. Renewal of protection is generally subject to payment of a renewal fee. However, unlike trademarks, industrial design protection, once granted, is not voidable if not actively used.

DRIGHT D'AUTHOR

Copyright protection covers original creations in the literary (including software), musical and artistic fields, regardless of the mode or form of expression. The acquisition of copyright protection is generally automatic as soon as your work is fixed on a material medium. However, in some cases it may be possible or, exceptionally, necessary to register the copyright.

Difficulties in Obtaining Intellectual Property Protection

Some of the difficulties that most SMEs face in obtaining intellectual property protection include:

- insufficient manpower to undertake the preparatory work necessary to obtain intellectual property protection, such as initial searches and other pre-filing procedures;

- high costs, particularly in the process of obtaining a patent, which may entail costs for the translation of documents and fees to be paid to intellectual property agents or lawyers;

- insufficient "in-house" knowledge of intellectual property rights and the procedures applicable to their protection.

To some extent, the burdens of obtaining IP protection can be reduced if you know more about the possibilities of using the IP system effectively. SMEs can also reduce the burden and costs of obtaining intellectual property protection by applying regional or international agreements when seeking protection abroad (see "Securing intellectual property rights of your SME abroad?"), using special services offered to SMEs where they exist or opting for lower levels of protection, such as protection by utility model, where the legislation of the of the countries in question provide for such forms of protection.

PROTECT THE INTELLECTUAL PROPERTY RIGHTS OF YOUR SME
To L'FOREIGN

Why have your SME's intellectual property protected abroad?

More and more small and medium-sized enterprises (SMEs) operate in more than one market, selling products or services or licensing or franchising their intellectual property rights and know-how beyond their national borders. However, intellectual property rights are territorial in nature, which means that they are generally protected only in the country or region of origin where protection was sought and obtained. This is why it is crucial to protect intellectual property rights on export markets, so as to benefit abroad from the same protection as on the local market.

QWHEN PROTECTING THE INTELLECTUAL PROPERTY OF YOURSMEAL'FOREIGNER?

As a general rule, you should ensure that your SME obtains appropriate protection as quickly as possible in all relevant export markets.

With regard to patents for inventions, most countries grant a priority period of 12 months from the date of filing of the first application for patent protection in other countries. After this period has elapsed, you may not be able to obtain patent protection in other countries, which may result in a significant loss of earnings in your exports (for a brief explanation of the meaning of the term “priority date”, see Frequently Asked Questions).

With regard to trademarks and industrial designs, most countries grant a priority period of six months from the date of filing of the first application for protection of a trademark or industrial design In other countries.

With regard to copyright, if you are a national or resident of a state party to the Berne Convention for the Protection of Literary and Artistic Works or a member of the World Trade Organization (WTO) and bound by the provisions of the TRIPS Agreement or if you published your work for the first time or at least simultaneously in one of the aforementioned countries, your copyright will automatically be protected in all other States which are parties to the Convention of Berne or who are members of the WTO.

VSHOW TO PROTECT THE INTELLECTUAL PROPERTY OF YOURSMEAL'FOREIGNER?

National requests

You have the option of applying for protection separately in different countries by filing the application directly with the national industrial property or intellectual property offices. Each request will eventually have to be translated into a prescribed language, usually the national language. You will need to pay national filing fees and, particularly for patents, you may be required to appoint an intellectual property agent or attorney to help you ensure that the application meets national requirements. If you are still in the phase of evaluating the commercial viability of an invention or are still looking for potential export markets or licensing partners, the national application procedure can seem particularly expensive and complicated, especially when protection is sought in a large number of countries. In this case, the possibilities offered by the international protection systems administered by WIPO for inventions, trademarks and industrial designs constitute another simpler and generally less costly solution.

Regional requests

Some countries have established regional agreements to protect intellectual property in an entire region through the filing of a single application. The regional intellectual property offices include:

European Patent Office(for European patents)

Office for Harmonization in the Internal Market(for trademarks and, in the future, industrial designs within the European Community)

African Regional Industrial Property Organization(ARIPO, the regional intellectual property office of English-speaking African countries for patents, trademarks and industrial designs)

African Intellectual Property Organization(OAPI, the regional intellectual property office of French-speaking African countries for patents, trademarks, industrial designs and, in the future, geographical indications and layout designs of integrated circuits)

Eurasian Patent Office(for patent protection in the Commonwealth of Independent States)

Benelux Trademark Office & Benelux Designs Office(for trademark and design protection in Belgium, the Netherlands and Luxembourg):

Patent Office of the Cooperation Council for the Arab States of the Gulf(for patents)

PPROTECTIONI N T E R N A T I O N A L

The international protection systems administered by WIPO significantly simplify the process of simultaneously applying for intellectual property protection in a large number of countries. Rather than filing national applications in several languages, you can, thanks to the international protection systems, file a single application, in a single language, by paying a single filing fee. Not only do these international filing systems facilitate the procedure, but they also considerably reduce, for trademarks and industrial designs, the cost of applying for international protection (for patents, the PCT allows you, within the framework of your SMEs, to save time in assessing the commercial value of your invention before paying national fees in the national phase).

International protection of inventionsis provided under the PCT system, the worldwide system for the simplified multiple filing of patent applications. By filing a single international patent application under the PCT, you are effectively seeking protection for an invention in a large number of countries (currently over 100) around the world.

International trademark protectionis provided for under the "Madrid system". The Madrid system considerably simplifies the procedure for registering a trademark in many countries party to this system. An international registration under the Madrid system produces the same effects as an application for registration of a mark filed in each country designated by the applicant and, unless refused by the office of a designated country within determined, this registration produces the same effects as if the registration had been made in the trademark registry of that country (see also "Twenty questions about the Madrid Protocol" (Adobe PDF)).

International protection of industrial designsis provided for under the Hague Agreement. This system offers the owner of an industrial design or model the possibility of obtaining protection for his design or model in several countries by filing a single application with the International Bureau of WIPO, drafted in a single language, and paying a single set of taxes in a single currency.

PWHY THE BRANDS ARE-THEY ESSENTIAL TO THE SUCCESS OF YOUR SME?

Your brands are, in many ways, the showcase of your business. They allow your customers to distinguish your products and services from those of your competitors, which gives your SME the opportunity to better market its products and services. However, trademarks are not only distinctive signs. They are also considered as a guarantee of stable quality. A customer who is satisfied with the quality of your product or service will continue to buy it, basing their expectations on the quality of the well-known brand. Therefore, you must take care in selecting and designing an appropriate mark, protecting it, using it in advertising, and fighting against its misleading or abusive use by others.

When choosing a mark, you should consider whether the mark you plan to use or similar marks have already been registered by other companies for the category of goods or services and for the markets in which you are interested. This type of information can be obtained by carrying out a search in the field of trademarks. It is crucial to carry out this research at an early stage to avoid unnecessary disputes with other companies and loss of resources.

After searching the trademark databases for the disputed trademarks, you need to think about the best way to protect your trademarks. For more information on the procedure for registering your trademark, see the section: "Some general indications on the procedures for registering trademarks".

For more on the importance of protecting your brand in export markets, see the following sections: "Using Trademarks and Designs to Market Products and Services to the abroad" and "Protecting the intellectual property rights of your SME abroad".

VSRRSP OR CHOOSE A BRAND

Creating or choosing a brand is not an easy task. There are, in fact, specialist companies whose main business is to find or develop a suitable brand that meets your needs. While there are no hard and fast rules as to what constitutes a successful brand, some useful guidelines have been developed. First, you need to make sure that the trademark you are considering meets the legal requirements for registering a trademark. Above all, your trademark must be distinctive enough to be protected and registered with the trademark office in your country and abroad. In addition, among the criteria generally used to create, design or choose a brand, you may wish to study some of them, in particular:

the sign must be easy to read, spell, pronounce and remember in all languages used;

IT MUST NOT HAVE NEGATIVE SLANG MEANINGS OR UNTOWARD CONNOTATIONS;

it should be suitable for export markets and should not have a negative meaning in foreign languages, especially if you plan to market the product abroad;

it must not create confusion as to the nature of the product.

it must be adaptable to all advertising media.

The brand you have chosen is likely to fall into one of the following categories:

Invented words (or "fancy" words): these are made up words that have no real meaning in any language (eg Kodak or Exxon). Coined words have the advantage of being easy to protect as they are more likely to be considered distinct. However, they may be more difficult to remember and for some consumers it will therefore be necessary to put more effort into advertising the products concerned.

Arbitrary marks: they consist of words that have a real meaning in a given language. However, the meaning of these words is not related to the product itself or any of its features (eg Apple (apple) for a computer). As with coined words, while the degree and facility of protection is generally high, there is no direct link between the mark and the product; therefore, it is necessary to use more elaborate commercial techniques to create this link in the mind of the customer.

Suggestive Marks: these are marks that allude to certain characteristics of the product. The advantage of suggestive marks is that they are a form of advertising and can create a direct link in the minds of customers between the mark, certain desired characteristics and the product. However, a related risk is that some jurisdictions may consider a suggestive mark to be too descriptive or not distinct enough to meet the criteria for obtaining trademark protection.

ECONDUCT A SEARCH IN THE FIELD OF TRADEMARKS

As a first step in protection, you are advised to carry out a trademark search to ensure that the trademark in question is not already in use by another business in the target market(s). s). In many countries, the trademark office registers trademarks without carrying out a comparison with registrations and applications for registration received before, leaving it to your future competitors to file an opposition after the publication or registration of the mark or request. Therefore, registering a trademark in these countries does not guarantee that the trademark will not infringe the rights of third parties. It is therefore important, where possible, to search national trademark databases,

Trademark searches can be carried out in online databases (although currently few countries offer these services) with the help of specialized companies or in the national trademark register. It is important to take into account that, while it is easy to distinguish marks identical to your own mark, it is more difficult to recognize potentially confusing marks which are in conflict with yours. Depending on the merits of the case, it may be useful to engage the services of a competent trademark agent or attorney to carry out a trademark search for your SME.

Since most marks (with the exception of "well-known marks") protect only the goods or services for which they are registered, as well as goods or services similar to those for which the mark is registered, the brand that you have registered can be used legally by third parties to market products or services that have no connection with those offered by your SME.

PROTECT YOUR SME'S BUSINESS SECRETS

What is a trade secret?

Generally speaking, any confidential business information that gives a business a competitive advantage can be considered a trade secret. Trade secrets include manufacturing or industrial secrets, as well as trade secrets. Unauthorized use of such information by persons other than the holder is considered an unfair practice and a violation of trade secrets. Depending on the legal system in force, the protection of trade secrets falls under the general principle of protection against unfair competition or is based on specific provisions or case law on the protection of confidential information.

The subject matter of trade secrets is generally defined broadly and includes sales methods, distribution methods, consumer profiles, advertising strategies, supplier and customer lists, and manufacturing processes. While ultimately the determination of what information is a trade secret depends on the particular circumstances of each case, it is clear that unfair practices with respect to confidential information include industrial or commercial espionage, breaking contract and breach of trust.

VSHOW TO PROTECT THE SECRETS OF'BUSINESS?

Unlike patents, trade secrets are protected without registration, ie trade secrets are protected without procedural formalities. Also, a business secret can be protected for an unlimited period. This is why the protection of trade secrets may seem particularly attractive for SMEs. However, certain conditions must be met for the information to be considered a trade secret. Bringing these conditions together can be more difficult and costly than it first appears. Although these conditions vary from country to country, some general standards are set out in Article 39 of the Agreement on Trade-Related Aspects of Intellectual Property Rights (TRIPS Agreement):

the information must be secret (in the sense that it is not generally known or readily accessible to persons in the circles which normally deal with the kind of information in question);

they must have commercial value because they are secret;

they must have been subject to reasonable arrangements on the part of the person who has lawful control of them to keep them secret (for example, by non-disclosure agreements).

Example

An SME develops a manufacturing process that allows it to obtain a better cost-effectiveness ratio. This process gives the company a competitive advantage. The company in question can therefore value its know-how as a business secret while wishing that its competitors do not know about it. It ensures that only a limited number of people know the secret and that those who do know are well aware of its confidential nature. When dealing with third parties or licensing its know-how, the company signs non-disclosure agreements to ensure that all parties know that the information is secret. In these circumstances, misappropriation of this information by a competitor or third party would be considered a breach of that company's trade secrets.

PRECAUTIONS MUST BE TAKEN BY YOURSME

SMEs make extensive use of trade secrets. In fact, many SMEs depend almost exclusively on trade secrets for the protection of their intellectual property (although often they are not even aware that trade secrets are protected by law). It is therefore important to ensure that companies take all necessary measures to effectively protect their trade secrets. These measures consist in particular of:

first, to determine whether the secret is patentable and, if so, whether it Gould not better protected by patent;

second, to ensure that only a limited number of people know about the secret and that they are all aware that it is confidential information;

third, to include non-disclosure agreements in employee contracts; however, in many countries, employees are bound by law to a duty of confidentiality to their employer, even in the absence of such agreements; the duty of confidentiality with respect to the secrets of the employer lasts in general, at least for a specified period, even after the employee has left his employment;

fourth, to sign non-disclosure agreements with partnersbusiness whenever confidential information is disclosed.

BCLAIMS OR SECRETS D'BUSINESS?

Trade secrets basically fall into two categories. On the one hand, trade secrets may relate to inventions or manufacturing processes which do not meet the patentability criteria and can therefore only be protected as trade secrets. This category could include customer lists or manufacturing processes that are not sufficiently inventive to warrant patenting (although they may be protected as utility models). On the other hand, trade secrets may relate to inventions which would meet the patentability criteria and could therefore be protected by a patent. In this case, the SME must make a choice: patent the invention or keep it as a business secret.

Advantages presented by trade secrets:

Trade secret protection has the advantage of not being limited in time (patents generally last up to 20 years). It can therefore continue indefinitely, as long as the secret has not been revealed to the public;

trade secrets do not incur a registration fee (although efforts to keep the information secret can come at a high cost);

BUSINESS SECRETS PRODUCE THEIR EFFECTS IMMEDIATELY;

the protection of trade secrets does not require compliance with certain formalities such as the disclosure of information to a government administration.

However, protecting confidential business information as a trade secret has some practical drawbacks, especially when the information meets patentability criteria:

if the secret is contained in an innovative product, third parties are likely to examine, disassemble and analyze it (i.e., "reverse engineer" it) in order to discover the secret and be able to then use it. In reality, the protection of the trade secrets of an invention does not give the exclusive right to prevent third parties from making commercial use of it;

once the secret is disclosed, anyone can access and use it at will;

a trade secret is more difficult to enforce than a patent. The level of protection granted to trade secrets varies considerably from one country to another, but is generally considered to be low, particularly compared to the protection offered by a patent;

a trade secret may be patented by a person other than the person who lawfully developed the relevant information.

VSAS IN WHICH IT CAN BE ADVANTAGEOUS FOR YOURSMETO PROTECT ITS SECRETS D'BUSINESS

Although all decisions are made on a case-by-case basis, trade secret protection is advisable in the following circumstances:

when the secret is not patentable;

where there is a strong likelihood that the information may be kept secret for an extended period of time. If the secret information consists of a patentable invention, trade secret protection is appropriate only if the secret can remain confidential for more than 20 years (the term of patent protection) and if third parties are not not likely to develop the same invention lawfully;

when the trade secret is not considered to have such value that it needs to be patented (although a utility model is a satisfactory solution in countries where utility model protection exists) ;

WHERE THE SECRET RELATES TO A MANUFACTURING PROCESS RATHER THAN A PRODUCT, THE PRODUCTS BEING MORE LIKELY TO BE BONELESS;

when you have filed a patent application and are awaiting grant of the patent.

However, it is important to take into account the fact that trade secret protection is generally weaker in most countries, that the conditions of protection and its scope can vary significantly from one country to another depending on existing statutory mechanisms and case law and that courts may require substantial and possibly costly efforts to maintain confidentiality. Patent or utility model protection, where possible, provides more secure protection.

HOW CAN YOUR SME BENEFIT FROM COPYRIGHT PROTECTION?

Is your company engaged in the creation, recording, publication, broadcast, distribution or retail sale of artistic, musical or literary works? Does your business have a website, publish a brochure, run a promotional video, or run advertisements in newspapers or on television? Does your SME use third-party music, images or software in its publications, brochures, databases or websites? Does your company own the rights to computer software? If the answer to any of the questions posed above is "yes", you may want to learn more about copyright issues.

When you better understand the basics of copyright protection, you may want to know what your small business needs to do to:

a) lawfully use or exploit the works or creations of third parties with the authorization of the author or right holder under fair and reasonable conditions;

b) protect your own works or creations and ensure that you make the best use of your right and rightfully receive financial compensation for any use of your creations.

DRIGHTS D'AUTHORS AND RELATED RIGHTS

What is copyright?

Copyright designates all the rights enjoyed by creators over their literary and artistic works.

What works are protected by copyright?

Works protected by copyright include, in particular, literary works (novels, poems, plays, reference works, newspapers and software), databases, films, musical compositions and choreographic works, artistic works such as as paintings, drawings, photographs and sculptures, architecture, and advertising creations, geographical maps and technical drawings.

What rights does the author have?

The creators of works protected by copyright and their heirs have certain fundamental rights. In particular, they have the exclusive right to use the work or to authorize its use under agreed conditions. The creator of a work may prohibit or authorize:

- its reproduction in various forms, for example in the form of printed matter or sound recordings;
- its performance in public, for plays or musical works, for example;

its recording, for example in the form of compact discs, cassettes or video cassettes;

its broadcasting by radio, cable or satellite;

its translation into other languages or its adaptation, consisting for example of turn a novel into a film script.

Many creative works protected by copyright require massive efforts in terms of distribution, communications and financial investment to be disseminated (for example, publications, sound recordings and films) : also the creators often sell their rights on their works to natural persons or to companies better equipped to market the works in return for a remuneration. This remuneration, which is often subordinated to the actual use of the work, is called copyright royalties.

These economic rights have a limited duration, according to the relevant WIPO treaties, to 50 years after the death of the creator. Some national laws provide for a longer period long. This limitation of the term of protection allows creators and their heirs to derive financial benefits from the work for a reasonable period of time. Copyright protection also includes moral rights, including the right to claim authorship of a work, and the right to oppose changes to the work that may damage the reputation of the creator. .

The creator - or holder of the copyright on a work - can assert his rights by addressing the administrative authorities and the courts to have the premises inspected in search of elements that will prove the production or possession of copies made illegally - "pirated" - of protected works. The holder may apply to the courts to put an end to these illegal activities, as well as to obtain compensation for the damage he has suffered in the form of loss of earnings and damage to his reputation.

Can ideas, procedures, methods or concepts be protected by copyright?

Copyright protection extends to expressions, not ideas, procedures, methods of operation, or mathematical concepts. This principle has been confirmed by the Agreement on Trade-Related Aspects of Intellectual Property Rights (TRIPS) of the World Trade Organization (WTO) as well asthe WIPO Treaty on the .

What are related rights?

A set of rights related to copyright has developed rapidly in these last 50 years. These rights, which have developed around works protected by copyright, are rights similar to copyright, but often more limited in scope and time, and possessed by:

performers(actors and musicians for example) on their performances;

sound recording producers(recordings on cassettes and compact discs) on their recordings;

- **broadcasting organizations**on their radio and television programs.

Why protect copyright?

Copyright and related rights are essential to human creativity because they provide creators with incentives in the form of moral recognition and fair compensation. Thanks to this system of rights, creators are sure that their works can be distributed without them having to fear unauthorized copying or piracy. This makes it possible to develop access to culture, knowledge and leisure everywhere in the world, and increases the enjoyment of them.

How has copyright adapted to technical progress?

The scope of copyright and related rights has widened enormously with the technical progress of the last decades, which has brought about new ways of disseminating creations by means such as global communication in the form of satellite broadcasting or compacts discs. The dissemination of works via the Internet is only the most recent stage of this evolution, which raises new questions concerning copyright. WIPO is actively participating in the ongoing international debate on the development of new standards for copyright protection in cyberspace. It administers the WIPO Copyright Treaty and the

What is the copyright regime?

The copyright itself is acquired without formalities. A work is considered protected by copyright as soon as it is created. However, many countries have a national copyright office, and some laws allow the deposit of works, for example the registration of titles.

Many owners of intellectual works do not have the means to take care of the legal and administrative defense of their copyright themselves, particularly in view of the worldwide increase in the use of rights in literary and musical works and in performances. As a result, collective management organizations or societies are increasingly being created in many countries. These societies can make their members benefit from their administrative and legal knowledge, for example with regard to the collection, management and payment of royalties due for the international use of their works.

What is the copyright regime? Is it necessary to register the copyright to benefit from the protection?

According to Berne Convention for the Protection of Literary and Artistic Works, the protection is automatic, in the sense that it does not require any filing or registration procedure for its existence. The author of an original work is protected from the creation of his work, without formality, in the States parties to the Berne Convention.
WIPO therefore does not offer a registration system for literary and artistic works.

However, many countries have a national office, and some countries provide for a registration procedure in their national legislation. In general, the registration of works can be used in court to establish the right of ownership.

VSPRACTICAL TIPS FOR YOURSMEAS'USER OF THE RIGHT D'AUTHOR

For some businesses, the use or exploitation of works, sound recordings, broadcasts, or interpretations or performances of copyrighted works is an essential part of day-to-day business. . This may be the case of broadcasting stations, publishing houses, libraries, shops or nightclubs. For other businesses, it may just be an occasional tool used to improve the company's publications, websites, and other ways of selling. For still others, the use of copyrighted material may be limited to that of their computer software. In all such cases, the following issues may need to be considered:

Do I need a license?Probably the most important thing for a business using or trading copyrighted works or related rights is whether a license is required to conduct those activities. As a general rule, any use or commercial exploitation of works protected by these rights is subject to the obtaining of a license or the transfer of the rights by the holder. This concerns activities as diverse as the use of a famous song in a television commercial, the sale or distribution of CDs and DVDs, or even the use of software in a company's computers. With respect to licensing, you must determine whether the rights are administered by a collective management organization or directly by the author or producer and negotiate a license agreement before using or exploiting a product. Remember that copyright infringement litigation can be very expensive and it would be wise to consider these issues before you get yourself and your business into trouble! You may also wish to benefit from advice on the clauses of your license agreement before signing it. For some products such as off-the-shelf software, the product is often licensed to you upon purchase. The terms and conditions of your license agreement are included in the packet, which you are free to return if you do not agree to them. Remember that copyright infringement litigation can be very expensive and it would be wise to consider these issues before you get yourself and your business into trouble! You may also wish to benefit from advice on the clauses of your license agreement before signing it. For some products such as off-the-shelf software, the product is often licensed to you upon purchase. The terms and conditions of your license agreement are included in the packet, which you are free to return if you do not agree to them. Remember that copyright infringement litigation can be very expensive and it would be wise to consider these issues before you get yourself and your business into trouble! You may also wish to benefit from advice on the clauses of your license agreement before signing it. For some products such as off-the-shelf software, the product is often licensed to you upon purchase. The terms and conditions of your license agreement are included in the package, which you are free to return if you do not agree to them. You may also wish to benefit from advice on the clauses of your license agreement before signing it. For some products such as off-the-shelf software, the product is often licensed to you upon purchase. The terms and conditions of your license agreement are included in the package, which you are free to return if you do not agree to them. You may also wish to benefit from advice on the clauses of your license agreement before signing it. For some products such as off-the-shelf software, the product is often licensed to you upon purchase. The terms and conditions of your license agreement are included in the packet, which you are free to return if you do not agree to them.

Is there a collecting society?Collecting societies greatly facilitate the process of obtaining licenses for several works. Rather than dealing directly with each author or rights holder, users have a centralized source through collective management societies where they can negotiate rates and terms of use and where they can obtain permissions easily and quickly. In recent years, the emergence of one-stop centers bringing together several collecting societies that can issue authorizations easily and quickly is considered particularly useful for multimedia productions for which a whole series of authorizations is necessary. Dealing with collecting societies where possible can save you a lot of time and money. You can obtain more information about collecting societies operating in your country from your country's copyright office.

Can you freely use works published on the Internet?It is often mistakenly believed that works published on the Internet are in the public domain and can therefore be freely used by anyone without the permission of the right holder. Any work protected by copyright or related rights, whether musical compositions, multimedia products, newspaper articles or audiovisual productions, for which the protection period has not expired, benefits of this protection, whether it is published on paper or on another medium, for example, the Internet. In any event, you should generally seek permission from the copyright holder before using the work. Similarly, authorization is required if your SME is dedicated to the publication or distribution on its website of works, sound recordings,

VSUSEFUL TIPS FOR YOURSMEAS A HOLDER OF THE RIGHT D'AUTHOR

If your company is directly in the copyright industry, that is, if it creates, publishes, records, distributes or sells works protected by copyright or related rights, make sure understand your rights and take all appropriate measures to exercise, license and enforce them. But, even if you are not directly related to the copyright industry, your company may occasionally produce works protected by copyright or related rights. Corporate publications, brochures, websites, television or print advertisements, or promotional videos are all subject to copyright protection. .

In any case, if you believe that your company has created works protected by copyright or related rights and you want them to derive the maximum benefit from them, it would be prudent to seek advice from your national copyright office or a specialized lawyer. The following questions may help you better understand the copyright regime in your country.

Is there a copyright register?Generally, copyright protection is automatic and does not depend on registration. In some countries, however, there is a copyright register, and it would be a good idea to register your work there, as this would be of great help in the event of a dispute over the ownership of the work by example.

Who owns the rights?The owner of copyright in a work is usually the original creator or author of the work. This rule, however, has a few exceptions. In some countries, for example, the economic rights in a protected work are deemed to belong initially to the employer or producer, while in other countries they are deemed to be assigned or transmitted to them. It would therefore be desirable to inform you about the regulations applicable in this respect in your country.

What are my rights?The exclusive rights granted to authors and other owners under national copyright laws vary from country to country. It can be said, however, that as a general rule exclusive rights include, for example, the right of reproduction (right to make copies of the work), the right of public performance, the right of broadcasting and the right adaptation. More and more countries are also recognizing rights holders over the distribution of their works on the Internet and providing them with protection against the circumvention of technological protection measures. It would therefore be interesting to know the rights provided by the copyright legislation of your country so that your SME can fully benefit from the protection of copyright and related rights. To facilitate the legitimate trade of protected works, it is also necessary to take into account the fact that under the terms of the WIPO treaties the economic rights granted to authors have a limited duration of 50 years after the death of the author. Longer periods of protection may be provided at national level. Collective management organizations are usually able to provide information on this. Also remember that copyright protection generally extends to moral rights, i.e. the right to claim authorship of the work and the right to oppose modifications that may harm the reputation of the creator. . account must also be taken of the fact that, under the terms of the WIPO treaties, the economic rights granted to authors have a limited duration of 50 years after the death of the author. Longer periods of protection may be provided at national level. Collective management organizations are usually able to provide information on this. Also remember that copyright protection generally extends to moral rights, i.e. the right to claim authorship of the work and the right to oppose modifications that may harm the reputation of the creator. . account must also be taken of the fact that, under the terms of the WIPO treaties, the economic rights granted to authors have a limited duration of 50 years after the death of the author. Longer periods of protection may be provided at national level. Collective management organizations are usually able to provide information on this. Also remember that copyright protection generally extends to moral rights, i.e. the right to claim authorship of the work and the right to oppose modifications that may harm the reputation of the creator. .

HASOTHER PRACTICAL TIPS FOR YOURSMEAS A HOLDER OF THE RIGHT D'AUTHOR

How do I get my works protected internationally? If the country of which you are a national or in which you reside has ratified the international conventions in the field of copyright and related rights administered by WIPO, such as the Berne Convention, or that country is a member of the World Trade Organization (WTO) and has complied with its obligations under the TRIPS Agreement, or if you made your work public for the first time or at least simultaneously in a country fulfilling the above criteria, your copyrighted work will automatically be protected in a large number of countries. If this is not the case, certain bilateral agreements between your country and other countries may provide for similar rights.

How can I license my works?If you want to license your work to users such as broadcasters, publishers, or even entertainment establishments of all kinds, such as bars or nightclubs, joining a collecting society can be a good option. Collective management organizations supervise the use of works on behalf of their creators and are responsible for negotiating licenses and collecting royalties. They are particularly widespread in the field of literary and artistic works where there may be a large number of users of the same work and where it would be difficult for both the right holder and the users to request specific authorization for each use and supervise the management of rights. Where collecting societies do not exist, license contracts must be negotiated individually with the licensee. The advice of a specialist can be useful to obtain advantageous conditions in the license agreement.

How do I enforce my rights?The creator of a work has the right to authorize or prohibit the use of his work. If someone uses your copyrighted works without permission, you can enforce your rights administratively and in court. In many countries, measures commonly known as border measures, intended to prevent the importation of pirated goods, are also applied. Advice from an intellectual property agent or lawyer, the copyright office or customs officials can be very helpful if you find that your rights to your works are being infringed (see also the section "How can your SME resolve intellectual property disputes?"). Certain works, such as software, phonograms and audiovisual works may include technical protection devices (eg encryption, restricted access systems) which protect them from unauthorized use. These systems are means for rights holders to limit access to their works to customers who accept the terms of use and the payment required for such use.

HOW CAN YOU USE COLLECTIVE MARKS, CERTIFICATION MARKS AND GEOGRAPHICAL INDICATIONS FOR THE BENEFIT OF YOUR SME?

It's not easy for small and medium-sized enterprises (SMEs) to make a name for themselves with consumers and retain customers. Regardless of the quality of the products on offer, accessing retail stores, local markets and distribution networks and getting consumers to know one's products are all steps that require a significant investment, often exceeding the budget of companies. As they are produced on a small scale, many SMEs find it difficult to mount an effective marketing campaign that allows them to position their products and give them a reputation that can attract consumers. That being so, what choices do they have?

"If you can't win, ally with your opponent," an old saying wisely goes. By acting together, SMEs can develop a common marketing campaign for their products using collective marks. Indeed, for many, one of the big problems encountered by SMEs is not so much their size but their isolation. Thanks to collective marks, different SMEs producing similar products have a solid basis for association and it is then easier for them to make a name for themselves and acquire notoriety for their products.

SMEs can also ask to register a geographical indication for their product if they consider that there is a clear link between it and the geographical area where it is manufactured. They will then be granted the exclusive right to use the indication (eg "champagne" or "tequila") to promote their product.

Finally, SMEs can use certification marks to certify that the product meets certain established standards, which indicates to consumers that the product has been checked by an organization deemed competent to certify the product and that it conforms to established standards. Certification marks can help a company market its products and improve its image to consumers.

LCOLLECTIVE TRADEMARKS

Most countries have provisions in their intellectual property laws for the protection of collective marks. Collective marks are generally defined as signs used to distinguish the geographical origin, the material, the method of manufacture or any other common characteristic of the goods or services of the different companies that use them collectively. The holder can be either an association to which these companies belong or any other entity, including a public institution or a cooperative.

The entity owning the collective mark is required to ensure that its members comply with certain standards (usually set out in the regulations concerning the use of this mark). Thus, the latter has the function of informing the public of certain particular characteristics of the product for which it is used. In most countries, it is required that any application for registration of a collective mark be accompanied by a copy of the regulations governing the use of this mark.

Collective marks are often used to promote products characteristic of a given region. In some cases, the creation of this type of mark has not only allowed to market these products more easily at the national level – and, sometimes, internationally – but also offered local producers a framework for cooperation. Indeed, when they create a collective brand, they must develop certain criteria and standards and develop a common strategy. In this sense, collective brands can become powerful instruments of local development.

Let us take the specific example of products which may present certain characteristics specific to the producers of a given region and linked to the historical situation and socio-cultural of this region. A collective mark can be used to symbolize all these characteristics and serve as a basis for the marketing of the products in question, in the interest of all producers.

SMEs forming an association can therefore register a collective mark in order to jointly market their products and make them better known. The collective mark can be used together with the individual mark of the producer of a particular product. Businesses thus have a means of differentiating their own products from those of the competition while benefiting from the confidence that consumers place in the products or services offered under the collective mark.

Collective marks can therefore represent useful instruments for SMEs that will help them to overcome some of the obstacles linked to their small size and their isolation in the market.National industrial property offices are able to provide information

more detailed information on registration procedures and the use of collective marks and certification marks.

For a concrete example of the use of collective marks, please consult the case studies " .

LGEOGRAPHICAL INDICATIONS

What is a geographical indication?

A geographical indication is a sign used on products which have a precise geographical origin and which possess qualities or a notoriety due to this place of origin. Most of the time, a geographical indication consists of the name of the place of origin of the products. Agricultural products generally have qualities that derive from where they are produced and are influenced by specific local factors, such as climate and soil. For a sign to function as a geographical indication, national legislation must contain provisions to that effect and consumers must consider it as such. Geographical indications can be used for a wide variety of agricultural products; for example,

Can geographical indications only be used for agricultural products?

The use of geographical indications is not limited to agricultural products. These indications can also highlight the particular qualities of a product due to human factors present at the place of origin of the products, such as certain manufacturing and tradition. The place of origin can be a village or a city, a region or a country. For example, the noun "Switzerland" or the adjective "Swiss" is considered in many countries as a geographical indication for products that are manufactured in Switzerland, in particular for watches.

What is an appellation of origin?

A designation of origin is a special type of geographical indication, used on products which have a particular quality due exclusively or essentially to the geographical environment in which they are obtained. The notion of geographical indication includes designations of origin.

What is the role of a geographical indication?

A geographical indication highlights a specific place or region of production which determines the characteristic qualities of the product originating there. It is important that the product derives its qualities and reputation from this place. These qualities depending on the place of production, there is a specific "link" between the products and their original place of production.

Why should geographical indications be protected?

For consumers, geographical indications are used to determine the origin and quality of products. Many of them have acquired a significant reputation which, if not adequately protected, can be subject to misrepresentation by dishonest commercial operators. The misuse of geographical indications by unauthorized third parties is detrimental to legitimate consumers and producers. The former are deceived because they are led to believe that they are buying an authentic product with specific qualities and characteristics when it is a worthless imitation. Legitimate producers, on the other hand, are harmed because they lose the benefit of lucrative business operations and the reputation of their products is damaged.

What is the difference between a geographical indication and a trademark?

A trademark is a sign used by a company to distinguish its goods and services from those of other companies. It gives its owner the right to prevent third parties from using the mark. By referring to the geographical indication, consumers know that a product comes from such and such a place and has certain characteristics which are due to the place of production. It can be used by all producers whose products originate from the place designated by the geographical indication and possess the characteristic qualities.

How is a geographical indication protected?

Geographical indications are protected under the provisions of national laws and a wide range of principles: for example, laws relating to unfair competition, laws relating to the protection of consumers, laws relating to the protection of certification or laws specifically protecting geographical indications or appellations of origin. Basically speaking, people who are not authorized to do so cannot use geographical indications if such use would mislead the public as to the true origin of the product. Penalties range from a court order prohibiting unauthorized use to damages and a fine or, in serious cases, imprisonment.

How are geographical indications protected internationally?

A number of treaties administered by the World Intellectual Property Organization (WIPO) aim to protect geographical indications; these are in particular the Paris Convention for the Protection of Industrial Property, of 1883, and the Lisbon Agreement for the Protection of Appellations of Origin and their International Registration. In addition, Articles 22 to 24 of the Agreement on Trade-Related Aspects of Intellectual Property Rights (TRIPS) deal with the international protection of geographical indications within the framework of the World Trade Organization (WTO).

What is a "generic" geographical indication?

If a geographical term is used to designate a type of product rather than to indicate the place of origin of this product, this term loses its function of geographical indication. When this is the case in a given country for a sufficiently long period, this country can accept that consumers consider that a geographical term which previously indicated the origin of the product (for example, the expression "Dijon mustard" associated with mustard from the city of Dijon in France) now designates a certain type of mustard, regardless of the place of production.

What is WIPO's role in the protection of geographical indications?

WIPO is responsible for administering a number of international agreements dealing, in particular or exclusively, with the protection of geographical indications (see, in particular, the Paris Convention for the Protection of Industrial Property and the Lisbon Agreement concerning the protection of appellations of origin and their international registration). In addition, within the framework of the Standing Committee on the Law of Trademarks, Industrial Designs and Geographical Indications, made up of representatives of Member States and interested organizations, WIPO is studying new ways of strengthening the protection of geographical indications in the international level.

LCERTIFICATION MARKS

Several countries also provide protection for certification marks. Certification marks are generally granted to products that meet defined standards but are not restricted to members of an entity. They can be used by anyone who can certify that the products in question meet certain established standards. Among the most famous certification marks we must mention the WOOLMARK label, which certifies that the products on which it is affixed are made of pure wool.

In many countries, the main difference between collective marks and certification marks is that the former can only be used by a specific group of companies, for example members of an association, while the latter can be used by anyone who meets the criteria defined by the trademark holder.
Registration of a certification mark is subject to an important requirement: the entity applying for it must be considered "competent to certify" the products concerned.

The certification mark can be used together with the individual mark of the producer of a particular product. The label used as a certification mark will be proof that the company's products meet the specific standards required for the use of this mark.

HOW TO GET INNOVATIONS PROTECTED BY UTILITY MODELS?

What is a utility model?

A utility model is an exclusive right granted for an invention and which allows the right holder to prevent the commercial use of the protected invention by third parties, without his authorization, for a limited period. In the definition which is generally given and which may vary from one country (where this type of protection is granted) to another, a utility model is likened to a patent. Indeed, utility models are sometimes referred to as "petty patents" or "utility certificates".

The main differences between utility models and patents relate to the following points:

The requirements for obtaining a utility model are less stringent than for patents. If the criterion of "novelty" must be met, the requirement of "inventive step" or "non-obviousness" may be less important or even non-existent. In practice, utility model protection is often requested for innovations of a rather complementary nature, which may not meet the patentability criteria.

The duration of utility model protection is shorter than that granted to patents and varies from country to country (generally between 7 and 10 years without the possibility of extension or renewal).

In most countries where utility model protection is granted, patent offices do not examine applications on the merits before registration. This means that the registration procedure is often noticeably simpler and faster and takes an average of six months.

Utility models are much cheaper to obtain and maintain (see "Can your SME obtain and maintain intellectual property protection?").

In some countries, utility model protection can only be obtained in certain technical fields and only for products and not for processes.

Utility models are considered to be particularly suitable for SMEs which make "minor" improvements to existing products or slightly adapt them. Utility models are mainly used for mechanical innovations.

The recently introduced 'Innovation Patent' in Australia is the result of extensive research into the needs of small and medium-sized enterprises and aims to provide a 'low-cost entry point into the intellectual property system'. See the link to the press release in the national administrations of the
industrial property in Australia.

The possibility of benefiting from utility model protection exists only in a limited but not insignificant number of countries.

OU GET MODEL D'USEFULNESS?

At present, a limited but significant number of countries grant utility model protection. These include the following countries: Germany, Argentina, Armenia, Australia, Austria, Belarus, Belgium, Brazil, Bulgaria, China, Colombia, Costa Rica, Denmark, Spain, Estonia, Ethiopia, Russian Federation, Finland, France, Georgia, Greece, Guatemala, Hungary, Ireland, Italy, Japan, Kazakhstan, Kenya, Kyrgyzstan, Malaysia, Mexico, OAPI, Uzbekistan, Netherlands, Peru, Philippines, Poland, Portugal,
Republic of Korea, Republic of Moldova, Czech Republic, Slovakia, Tajikistan, Trinidad and Tobago, Turkey, Ukraine and Uruguay.

In countries where national law does not provide for utility model protection, SMEs can either apply for a patent (see "Can your SME obtain and maintain intellectual property rights?" and "How turn inventions into profitable assets for your SME?"), or keep the invention as a trade secret (see "Protecting your SME's trade secrets").

VSHOW TO MANAGE YOUR INTELLECTUAL PROPERTY ASSETS SME?

To manage the intellectual property assets of a company, it is not enough to simply obtain theoretical intellectual property rights from the intellectual property office of its country. The rights deriving from a patent or a trademark are of interest only if they are suitably exploited. Also, some of a company's high-value intellectual property does not require formal registration, but other protective measures may need to be taken (eg, non-disclosure agreements). Companies wishing to take full advantage of their know-how and creativity should take the necessary steps to develop an intellectual property strategy and seek to integrate it into their overall business strategy. In this regard, intellectual property issues should be taken into account when developing business plans and marketing strategies. A basic IP strategy should include at least the following elements:

A policy for obtaining intellectual property rights

A single product or service may be protected by different forms of intellectual property rights relating to different aspects of that product or service. SMEs should investigate the best form of protection and ensure that all theoretical rights are obtained as soon as possible (see "Can your SME obtain and maintain intellectual property protection?"). SMEs should also bear in mind that creating a comprehensive intellectual property portfolio can represent a considerable investment. This is especially true for patents.

A policy on the exploitation of intellectual property

There are several ways to exploit IP assets, including: commercializing IP-protected products and services; entering into license or franchise agreements; the sale of intellectual property assets to other companies; the creation of joint ventures; the use of intellectual property as a means of accessing the techniques of other companies through the conclusion of cross-license agreements; or the use of intellectual property to obtain financing for a company. Companies must decide in each case how to make the most of their intellectual property assets, both domestically and internationally.

A policy for monitoring intellectual property

It is important to regularly consult patent and trademark databases in order to keep abreast of recent developments in the technical field, to identify new licensing partners or suppliers, to define new business prospects, to monitor activities of competitors, to know potential infringers and to avoid infringing the rights of competitors. See also "How to use patent information for the benefit of your SME?" and "Perform a trademark search".

A policy on the enforcement of intellectual property rights

It is essential to have a clear policy on the enforcement of intellectual property rights, given the losses that may arise from the existence of infringement in the marketplace and large sums incurred in certain intellectual property disputes. See "How can your SME resolve intellectual property disputes?".

A description of the means used by different companies with different technical capacities to develop intellectual property strategies adapted to their needs can be found in a WIPO document devoted to "The management of intellectual property rights by small and medium-sized enterprises" (see document WIPO/ACAD/E/93/12 available in English in Adobe PDF format).

QPRACTICAL INTELLECTUAL PROPERTY ISSUES WHEN'ELABORATION OF'A DEVELOPMENT PLAN

What can a development plan do for you?

A business plan is a mechanism to ensure that a company's resources or assets are usefully employed in all activities in order to gain and maintain a competitive advantage in the market. For a new business it is a blueprint for success and for an existing business the plan provides an overview of where the business is, how it positions itself and seeks to achieve its goals for become or remain a successful business.

Developing a development plan takes a lot of work. So what justifies the time and energy you are going to put into developing a plan? A development plan can be used for several purposes:

Investigate the possibility of realizing your business idea: an established business plan obliges a company to consider all the essential questions, namely the potential demand for its products or services, the nature of the competition, the barriers to entry, the axis of the specific commercial proposal of the new or improved products or services, the resources required, the necessary number of employees, the appropriate technologies and strategic partners, the search for financing, the expected start-up costs, the marketing strategies and others.

Get access to services and start-up funds: Business incubators and potential investors and funders require well-designed and realistic business plans. Since this is often not the case, it is no wonder that investors and business incubators reject 80% of the business plans they receive.

Provide strategic direction: A business plan is a reference document that provides you and your management team with an objective basis for determining whether your business is on track to achieve its goals within the set time frame and with available resources.

Provide a standard or benchmark for evaluating business decisions and outcomes in the future. This standard or benchmark may evolve with the business and the development plan is, as such, a living document that needs to be revised based on new and changing circumstances.

Why should intellectual property be part of your development plan?

New or original knowledge and the creative expression of ideas is a driving force behind successful 21st century businesses. Therefore, the protection of such knowledge and creative expressions from inadvertent disclosure or unauthorized use by competitors plays an increasingly critical role in gaining and maintaining competitive advantage. Starting a business also requires various other types of resources, including a network of contacts and funds. The intellectual property protection system is a key instrument to 1) ward off unscrupulous competitors, 2) strengthen relationships with employees, consultants, suppliers, contractors, business partners and customers, and
3) obtain funds.

To be accepted by a business incubator or to attract investors, it is necessary to have a quality development plan that objectively presents the prospects of the proposed business. To convince investors, you must demonstrate 1) that there is a demand for your product in the market, 2) that your product is better than competing products, if any, and 3) that you have taken the adequate measures to prevent your success from being "parasitized" by dishonest competitors.

Most entrepreneurs would claim that the product they offer is innovative, unique, or superior to competitors' offerings. But is this really the case? If you think so, you have to prove it, and a patent (or the results of a reliable patent search) may be your best proof of novelty.

Trade names, trademarks and domain names can be the essential elements in distinguishing your product from those of competitors. Therefore, the trade name, trademark(s) and domain name(s) you offer should be chosen carefully and the steps taken to register them should be mentioned in your business plan.

In addition, service providers to new high-tech companies and investors will want to be sure that the product you are offering to sell does not rely unduly on trade secrets, copyrighted content, patents or other intellectual property rights belonging to other companies, which could cause your own company to collapse following costly lawsuits. In some cutting-edge industries, the risk of infringement of third-party intellectual property rights is high, and tech start-up service providers and investors may be reluctant to engage unless you prove the absence of risk (for example by means of a patent or trademark search).

For many companies, confidential business information (such as production information, secret inventions, as well as technical, financial and marketing know-how) can alone create a competitive advantage. Under such conditions, it is important to inform tech start-up service providers and investors that your company has important trade secrets (known as trade secrets) and that you have taken adequate steps to protect them. employees and competitors.
In fact, even the development plan itself is a secret document to which access should be selective and generally permitted only after the employee has signed a non-disclosure or confidentiality agreement. , the investor or any other relevant person.

In short, if intellectual property is an important asset for your business (i.e. if you own patents or patentable techniques, industrial designs, trade secrets, recognized trademarks or if you are a rights holder heritage on protected works), it must represent an essential aspect of your development plan. The proper disclosure of a company's assets and market opportunities should not only list tangible assets (e.g. plants, equipment, capital, etc.) but also intangible assets since the latter constitute more moreover the key to the success of companies in an extremely competitive environment. As such, any indication confirming your due diligence in managing intellectual property assets is likely to go a long way in convincing tech start-up service providers and investors that your company has potential.

How can intellectual property be integrated into the development plan development process?

Writing a plan requires good preparation. You must first consider a number of questions. You need to know the nature of your business, know what resources are needed to achieve the objectives, identify your target markets, assess the solidity and the possibilities of growth of the business etc. Additionally, you should determine the commercial utility of intellectual property assets, whether owned by you or licensed by another company, and the resources required to acquire and maintain those assets.

The discussion below lists some key questions about IP aspects that you need to consider when developing your business plan. The different points will be more or less important depending on your particular situation and your activities. Moreover, this list is not exhaustive, many other aspects must be taken into consideration according to your particularities. However, the answers to these questions can help you integrate IP assets into the process of developing your business plan.

1. What intellectual property assets do you hold?

Define and categorize your intellectual property portfolio. This always contains confidential information or business secrets, one or more trade names and one or more trademarks, it also often contains domain names, industrial designs or models, titles of copyright and rights related products, and sometimes utility models and patents.

What other intangible assets do you have? In this regard, also take into consideration franchise, license and distribution agreements, publication rights, non-competition clauses, information databases, computer software, commercial profile, knowledge of management, distribution network, technical skills, etc.

2. What is the status of your intellectual property portfolio?

Do you have a system for determining your intellectual property assets?

Do you hold an intellectual property portfolio? When was it created? By who?

Which of your intellectual property assets are subject to registration? Are they registered or should they be? Are they also registered in foreign countries or in export markets? Does the registration need to be renewed? If yes, when?

Do you carry out management checks of your intellectual property or do you plan to do so? If so, how often and who is responsible for it?

3. How do you plan to protect your intellectual property assets?

If you commercialize your intellectual property assets (whether individually or with a partner), do you benefit from arrangements that guarantee ownership or co-ownership?

If you subcontract part of your commercial activities, have you established contracts guaranteeing your intellectual property rights on the subcontracted work and prohibiting third parties from profiting from your products or marketing them without your prior agreement?

How easy or difficult is it for others to obtain or properly reproduce your secret business information? What steps are taken to ensure the secrecy of your confidential business information?
Do you have an integrated security policy and plan for your physical and electronic assets? If you market your intellectual property assets (whether personally or with a partner), do you have arrangements in place to ensure the confidentiality of your secret business information?
Have you introduced confidentiality or non-disclosure clauses and non-competition clauses in the employment contracts of your key employees and agreements with your business partners?

Have you ensured that confidential business information or trade secrets are not made available or disclosed by posting on or through your website? Are all your URL headers free of confidential information? Do your web pages contain links to pages hosting confidential information?

4. What is the role of IP assets in the success of your business?

To what extent are your IP assets actually used or potentially useful, or no longer used by your business?

Does the commercial success of your business depend on intellectual property assets, whether owned or licensed by your business? What types of intellectual property assets are these?

Do you have new products or processes that will give you a unique competitive advantage? If so, will they revolutionize an industrial sector? Can the related intellectual property rights be secured to provide additional differentiation and prevent competitors from entering the market?

What competitive advantage do your intellectual property assets (owned or licensed) give your business? Evaluate and explain the extent to which the intellectual property provides customer interest and contributes to the acquisition of a sustainable competitive advantage.

Are your trade secrets, patents, trademarks, copyrighted works and industrial designs enough to protect the elements of your business that determine its success?

5. Do you own all the IP assets you need or are you dependent on IP assets held by third parties?

Do you own the intellectual property assets you use? Can you prove it? Do you have records, records, contracts, and other evidence that an investor, business partner, or court may require? Have you identified complaints that third parties may file regarding your intellectual property titles (for example, industrial sponsors or beneficiaries of research contracts)?

Are you sure you are not infringing the intellectual property rights of a third party? Can you prove it (eg have you done a patent, trademark or industrial design search)? Have you verified that none of your key employees who have worked for a competitor in the past are bound by non-competition or confidentiality and non-competition agreements? post-employment non-disclosure with a previous employer? Do you need access to third party intellectual property to exploit your business idea? Have you been granted the licenses you need to use the intellectual property that you do not own?

Have you signed non-disclosure or non-competition agreements with key members of your staff, contractors, consultants or other outside vendors who transfer to your company any intellectual property they create when do they work for you?

When you use outside vendors to write and design your marketing or advertising materials or your website and web pages, do the contracts specify who owns the intellectual property created as part of this? If employees initiate a creation, is it within the scope of their duties? If not, have you provided a written deed of assignment of the copyright and other intellectual property rights concerned? Do you have proper permissions to use, on your website or otherwise, written materials, designs, photographs, music or anything else created by a third party?

Does your website contain meta tags, hyperlinks, frames or other strong links to other websites? Have the third parties concerned duly given their authorization for this?

6. Do you have sufficient knowledge of your competitors' IP strategies and IP portfolios?

Do you have a plan for gathering competitive information? Do you collect IP information and databases or plan to use them to gain insights to be more competitive than your competitors? By searching patent, trademark, and industrial design registers, you can obtain detailed legal, technical, and business information about a competitor's operations and products. You can use this information to estimate if there might be a market for your products. In addition, an intellectual property search allows you to check whether you can protect your intellectual property,

Are there any intellectual property barriers preventing you from entering your competitor's market, such as patents, trademarks or industrial designs, highlighting consumer loyalty to the competitor's image and brands, etc.?

7. Do you have an intellectual property policy and strategy in place for your company?

How do you generally identify, protect, exploit and manage your intellectual property assets?

What projects have you put in place to derive the maximum benefit from the commercialization of your intellectual property assets?

Do you have a particular marketing strategy? Do you plan to export? If yes, do you use or do you plan to use a regional or international filing or registration system (such as the Patent Cooperation Treaty, Madrid System or Hague Agreement) for applications patent and trademark or design registrations?

Have you evaluated the possibilities of commercializing all or part of your intellectual property assets wholly or partially through licensing, franchising or sales?

Have you submitted your intellectual property to independent management review on a regular basis? Have your intellectual property assets been valued? Was it done independently?

To what extent have you considered tax issues and incentives associated with commercializing your intellectual property? This operation may be subject to prior tax conditions (eg registration). The taxation regime for income and expenses arising from the commercialization of your intellectual property may deviate significantly from the accounting system. Government financial assistance measures can be applied to intellectual property assets and their commercialization.

Do you plan to use your intellectual property assets as collateral or security for a loan or to establish a tradable title in the securities market?
What are the possibilities for securitizing future revenue streams related to a group or portfolio of intellectual property assets owned by you?

Do you have a staff training program covering the management and protection of your intellectual property assets?

Business plans are an essential tool for engaging tech start-up service providers and investors and exploring opportunities for your business. Because intellectual property gives your business competitive advantages and increases its value, it is necessary to make your intellectual property assets known to new high-tech business service providers and investors by integrating them appropriately into your plan. of development.

QA FEW IMPORTANT ELEMENTS TO TAKE INTO CONSIDERATION WHEN TUNING A'AN INTELLECTUAL PROPERTY STRATEGY

Check trademark databases to avoid using an existing trademark and protect trademarks before launching a new product or service under a new brand. In this regard, it is important to consider export markets and to avoid using a mark that may have a negative meaning in a foreign language.

Identify patentable subject matter and ensure that it is patented early enough to avoid losing the invention to competitors.

Ensure, before filing a patent application, that patentable inventions are not shared with third parties or have not been published. To meet patentability criteria, inventions must be considered "new". Early disclosure of an invention (for example, by publication) will compromise the chances of the invention being considered novel and therefore patentable.

Ensure that trade secrets are kept secret within the company and develop, where appropriate, non-disclosure agreements when negotiating and sharing information with business partners, in order to protect business secrets.

For export-oriented companies, ensure that intellectual property is protected in all potential export markets. With regard to patents, it is important to bear in mind that a company generally has 12 months to from the filing date of a national application to file the same patent application in other countries.

Use your intellectual property portfolio as a bargaining chip when seeking sources of financing for your business (for example, include intellectual property assets, especially patents, utility models, and industrial designs in your business plans, because they can help you convince investors of the business opportunities available to your company).

Use patent information available in patent databases to develop your business strategies.

Where research is conducted jointly with other companies or research institutes, ensure that ownership of potential intellectual property assets created by the research project is clearly identified.

Monitor the market and ensure that your intellectual property assets are not harmed. If your intellectual property rights are violated, you are advised to consult a lawyer (see also “How can your SME resolve intellectual property disputes?”).

If you are unsure of the best way to protect your company's intangible assets, having your IP assets audited can be a first step in the right direction, in order to identify all the information relevant to your company and to bring it to light. develop an intellectual property strategy. Sometimes companies are not aware of the value of the assets they possess in the form of information, innovative ideas and know-how and do not take the necessary measures to protect them.

This list is by no means exhaustive. It summarizes some fundamental measures successfully implemented by companies that have fully integrated intellectual property rights into their business strategy.

HASOTHER RELATED LINKS AND DOCUMENTS

“The management of intellectual property rights by small and medium-sized enterprises” (see document WIPO/ACAD/E/93/12 available in English in Adobe PDF format)

“The Role of Intellectual Property Rights in Promoting Competitiveness and Business Development” (see document WIPO/IPR/MCT/99/5.A available in English in Adobe PDF format)

“Strategies adopted by companies to manage, exploit and enforce their intellectual property rights” (see document WIPO/IP/PK/98/7 available in English in Adobe PDF format)

Connections

HOW TO USE PATENT INFORMATION IN THE BENEFIT OF YOUR SME?

What is "patent information"?

"Patent information" is the technical and legal information contained in patent documents which are regularly published by patent offices. A patent document includes the full description of how a patented invention works, the claims that determine the scope of protection, as well as information about who invented the invention, when it was patented, and relevant documentation. . About two-thirds of the technical information disclosed in patents has never been published elsewhere, and the total number of patent documents worldwide is around 40 million. Patent information therefore represents the most comprehensive collection of classified technical data.

PWHY L'PATENT INFORMATION PRESENTED-T-SHE AN INTEREST FOR YOURSME?

Patent information is of interest to your SME for a number of reasons. The most important is certainly that patents constitute a privileged source of technical information, which can be valuable for SMEs within the framework of the development of the company's strategic plan. Most inventions are first disclosed to the public when the patent (or, if the law so provides, when the patent application) is published. Also, patents constitute a source of information on the most recent research and innovations, often long before the innovative products appear on the market. The technical information contained in patent documents can provide your SME with valuable insights that it can use to:

avoid incurring unnecessary expenses in order to conduct research in a field Already known;

identify and evaluate techniques for licensing or technology transfer;

identify alternative techniques;

keep abreast of the latest techniques in his field of specialization;

find immediate solutions to technical problems;

come up with innovative ideas.

From the point of view of your company's business strategy, patent information helps you in particular:

find business partners;

find suppliers and materials;

to monitor the activities of actual and potential competitors;

identify thin markets.

Finally, SMEs can use the information contained in patent documents to:

avoid possible problems of infringement of the rights of third parties;

assess the patentability of their own inventions;

oppose the grant of patents if they conflict with their own patent.

QWHAT ARE THE ADVANTAGES OF PATENT DOCUMENTS AS A SOURCE OF INFORMATION?

They contain information that is often not disclosed in other types of publications.

They are presented in a relatively standardized form and include an abstract, bibliographic data, a description of the invention and, in most cases, drawings illustrating the invention, as well as complete information about the applicant.

They are classified according to technical field (for more information, see the document "General Information on the International Patent Classification System"; also available in French and Spanish).

They contain examples of possible applications of an invention in industry.

They cover almost all technical areas.

OU AND HOW TO GET L'PATENT INFORMATION?

The creation of web-based patent search databases has greatly facilitated access to patent information and reduced the cost of using it. Where web-based databases are not available, searchable databases can be searched manually, on microfilm or CD-ROM, at national patent offices or trade agencies.
Sources of patent information include:

the WIPO Intellectual Property Digital Library: ipdl.wipo.int (a comprehensive electronic database of international patent applications filed under the PCT system since 1997);

national patent offices: technical information services based on patent information are generally provided against payment of a fee;

patent agents/attorneys or commercial bodies;

manual searches in patent centres, libraries or national patent offices;

electronic searches in electronic databases or CD-ROMs.

Links to some free online patent databases

HASOTHER RELATED LINKS AND DOCUMENTS

"Patent Information and Documentation: Contents of a Patent Document" (see document WIPO/IP/CM/99/16 available in Adobe PDF format).

"Patent Documents as Sources of Technical Information" (see document WIPO/IP/ET/00/9 available in Adobe PDF format).

British Library Science Technology and Business (STB) Patent Information Services.

HOW TO LICENSE INTELLECTUAL PROPERTY RIGHTS? AN ESSENTIAL ELEMENT OF YOUR SME'S COMMERCIAL STRATEGY

You may be considering starting a new business, expanding an existing business (expanding its scope or business areas) or improving the quality of products or services provided by your SME, with a view to strengthen its position in the market. Often, the licensing of intellectual property rights is an effective tool for achieving these business objectives.

A license agreement is a collaboration between the owner of intellectual property rights (licensor) and a third party who is authorized to use these rights (licensee) against payment of an agreed amount (fee or royalty). There are various types of license agreements, which generally fall into one of the following categories:

technical license agreements

brand licenses and franchise agreements

license agreements

In practice, all or some of these contracts often form part of a single contract since transfers of this nature concern many rights and not just a single category of intellectual property right. You may also enter into license agreements in other circumstances, such as during a merger or acquisition or when negotiating a joint venture.

All of these mechanisms, whether used alone or in combination, offer your SME, as licensor or licensee, a whole range of possibilities for doing business in your country or abroad. As an IP owner and licensor, your SME can expand its business to the limit of its partner's business and secure a steady stream of additional revenue. As a licensee, your SME can manufacture, sell, import, export, distribute and market various products or services, activities that it could not possibly have carried out in other circumstances.

In the international context, a formal license agreement is only possible if the intellectual property right you wish to license is also protected in the other country or countries concerned. If your intellectual property right is not protected in such country or countries, not only will you not be able to license it, but you will also have no legal right to restrict its use by a third party.

VSLICENSING OF TECHNIQUES

If your SME is looking for:

to improve the quality of its products or to manufacture a new product by using the rights held by third parties in the form of a patent, utility model or know-how protected by a trade secret, the acquisition of these rights through a technology licensing agreement may be the right solution; Where

to enter or expand a market for a product for which it owns the patent, utility model or know-how rights protected by a trade secret, authorize a third party to use its techniques or product under a technology license agreement may be the right solution.

Under a technology license agreement, the licensor authorizes the licensee to use the technology under certain agreed conditions. It is therefore a contract freely concluded between two parties and whose clauses have been agreed.

joint ventures

A joint venture can refer to any type of business relationship between two or more companies that pool their resources in order to achieve a common business objective. Often, within the framework of such a contract, a part contributes to the project by bringing the techniques and the know-how which it has and the other part brings a financial contribution and its competences. Therefore, the joint venture often includes a license agreement between the parties involved to regulate the use of trade secrets and to provide compensation for their use.

VSFRANCHISING OR TRADEMARK LICENSE AGREEMENTS

If your SME is looking for:

to market a product or service and that the brand (trademark of goods or services) belongs to a third party; Where

to enter a market or to expand the existing market for the product or service for which your SME holds the rights conferred by a trademark,

consideration should be given to entering into a trademark licensing agreement or a franchise agreement.

The primary function of a trademark or service mark is to distinguish the goods and services supplied by one business from those supplied by another business, often allowing source to be identified and implicit reference to quality and to fame. This function is, to some extent, compromised if the trademark owner licenses another business the right to use the trademark under a trademark license agreement. Thus, it is advisable for the trademark owner, who often is required to do so by law or contract, to closely monitor the licensee to ensure that quality standards are met so as not to deceive the customer.

A franchise contract allows the holder of certain technical or other skills who generally enjoys a reputation linked to the use of a brand of products or services (the franchisor), to associate with another company (the franchisee) who will bring their skills or financial resources to provide products or services to the customer. The franchisor ensures, through the provision of technical skills and managerial skills, that the franchisee maintains quality and other standards in connection with the use of the brand of products or services which often require certain standardized characteristics such as, for example, for a commercial uniform.

VSRIGHTS LICENSE AGREEMENTS'AUTHOR

If your SME is looking for:

to manufacture, distribute or market the products of literary endeavors and artistic works of certain creators, or

- to penetrate a market or to enlarge the existing market for its literary and artistic products,

consideration should be given to entering into a copyright license agreement. Many rights holders find it difficult to manage their rights themselves and have formed collective management organizations that represent them and manage their rights. If you are interested in these rights, you can contact the appropriate collective management organization which is authorized to license the various rights of its members.

HASOTHER RELATED LINKS AND DOCUMENTS

National Technology Transfer Center (NTTC)
The NTTC is aimed particularly at the research industry and businesses in the United States of America, but contains tips on how to access unused technology lying dormant on laboratory shelves.

Intellectual Property Technology Exchange, Inc..
Founded in 1999, TechEx is a private company that allows the sale and purchase of emerging techniques in the biomedical field via the Internet. It is, however, a members-only system and restricted to authorized users such as licensing professionals and venture capitalists.

Technology New Zealand
This site aims to bring together the sources of technical advice available mainly on the Internet and, in particular, to provide advice for the negotiation of license agreements.

Intellectual Property Licensing Seminar of the University of Dayton School of Law
This site contains materials on various aspects of licensing.

HOW CAN YOUR SME RESOLVE INTELLECTUAL PROPERTY DISPUTES?

The more valuable your SME's intellectual property assets are, the greater the likelihood that third parties will want to use them, if possible, without paying. Do you have a strategy to stop them? If, despite your best efforts, someone imitates or copies your products or infringes your SME's intellectual property rights without your permission, what should you do? What are the possibilities open to you? How to evaluate the advantages and disadvantages of the different possible solutions? Or will you rush to take the case to court?

You have the possibility of "ignoring" the violation of the intellectual property rights of your SME if the loss of profits, the fall in turnover or the loss of profit seems negligible to you. If the degree of violation of rights is already high or is on the way to becoming so, then you need to find the culprits as soon as possible and take action against them quickly, but methodically. In other cases, however, you may be accused of stealing or violating a third party's intellectual property rights intentionally or without your knowledge.

In either case, it would be prudent, before taking any official action, to seek legal advice from a competent intellectual property professional in order to more accurately assess the possibilities for your SME to obtain a favorable result, at a lower cost. The cost can be calculated according to the time taken to obtain this decision, the legal costs and the lawyer's fees which you will have paid and the direct and indirect costs induced by the other solutions which you will have to study in the event of a decision. negative. You must also assess your chances of winning your case, the amount of compensation and damages that you can reasonably obtain from the offender,

It is obvious that in both cases it is important to carefully evaluate the advantages and disadvantages of the various possible solutions.

HASRESOLUTION AND MEDIATION

In many cases, the most expensive way to fight an infringement of intellectual property rights may be to initiate legal proceedings in a court that has jurisdiction over the matter, particularly when the infringement has been brought by several " competitors" under the same or different jurisdictions. In the latter case, your SME will have to enforce its rights in different places, before different courts. This is why it would possibly be desirable to resort to an out-of-court dispute resolution mechanism, which is generally less expensive and less time-consuming for your SME. Moreover, mediation is particularly advantageous because, often,

Judicial procedure or out-of-court dispute resolution?

Depending on the merits of the case, mediation (conciliation) or arbitration may be a satisfactory method of alternative dispute resolution. However, these alternatives can generally only be applied if the dispute over intellectual property rights is between two parties to a contract, for example, a licensor and a licensee, or partners in a joint venture, which have agreed to resort to mediation or arbitration in preference to a judgment rendered by a competent court. It is prudent, when drawing up the initial contract, to consider the possibility of a dispute and to provide for the means of settling it. Once a dispute has arisen, it is more difficult, if not impossible, to reach an agreement through mediation or arbitration.

Your SME may, however, wish to use the possibility of asking the WIPO Arbitration and Mediation Center to contact the other company with which it is in dispute in order to encourage the parties to submit the dispute to it with a view to settlement under the WIPO Mediation, Arbitration or Expedited Arbitration Rules. Often, mediation and arbitration are a very good alternative to traditional legal proceedings or at least, in the case of mediation, a less expensive first step. As part of its business strategy, your SME would benefit from including appropriate clauses in contracts so that it can settle, if necessary,

The WIPO Arbitration and Mediation Center

Among the many bodies your SME can turn to for help in resolving a dispute, without resorting to legal proceedings, is the WIPO Arbitration and Mediation Center, which offers a variety of settlement of commercial disputes between private companies, including SMEs; it has been particularly effective in resolving domain name disputes.

The WIPO Arbitration and Mediation Center website contains a detailed description of the benefits of mediation or arbitration and the various services provided.

FRESPECT THE INTELLECTUAL PROPERTY RIGHTS OF YOURSME

It is useless to obtain and preserve an intellectual property right if this right cannot be sanctioned in the market. It is the threat of sanction that makes it possible to exploit an intellectual property right as a commercial asset. In this context, the existence of an effective sanctions regime becomes a central aspect of a well-functioning intellectual property system.

Why enforce intellectual property rights?

The main objective of intellectual property protection is to allow your SME to reap the benefits of the inventions and creations of its employees that have made it possible to obtain intellectual property rights. These intellectual property assets can only be beneficially exploited if the intellectual property rights can be sanctioned because otherwise the infringers will always take advantage of the absence of effective sanction mechanisms to take advantage of the considerable work that has been done. In summary, it is fundamental for your SME to enforce its intellectual property rights, in order to:

preserve the legal validity of its intellectual property rights with competent public authorities;

prevent the occurrence or continuation of any infringement of those rights in the marketplace, in order to avoid harm, including loss of goodwill or reputation;

seek compensation for actual harm, for example, loss of profit arising from a market rights infringement case.

SACTION–TO WHOM THE'INITIATIVE?

The burden of enforcing intellectual property rights lies primarily with the rights holder. It is up to your SME, as the rights holder, to identify any violation/infringement of its intellectual property rights and to decide on the measures to be taken. While in most cases it is civil lawsuits that are incurred, in the event of counterfeiting and piracy, you can consider criminal proceedings if this possibility exists.

However, national or state governments have the responsibility to put in place bodies that facilitate the enforcement of intellectual property rights. The judiciary and, in some cases, administrative bodies such as intellectual property offices or customs authorities, are governmental institutions that may be responsible for combating infringement or counterfeiting. When border measures are taken to prevent the importation of counterfeit branded goods or pirated goods, the customs administration has a fundamental role to play in enforcing intellectual property rights at the national borders of your country. In accordance with the provisions of the applicable legislation, the customs administration must take action, on its own initiative, at the request of the right holder or it must comply with a court order. In addition, in some countries, associations in the industrial sector help their members to enforce their intellectual property rights (see the following addresses: Where.

HASACCESSIBILITY OF SANCTION PROCEDURES

The Agreement on Trade-Related Aspects of Intellectual Property Rights (TRIPS Agreement) obliges members of theWorld organization of commerce (industrialized countries and many developing countries) to implement the mechanisms provided for the enforcement of intellectual property rights. The relevant provisions of the TRIPS Agreement seek to ensure that civil, administrative and criminal procedures and remedies meet prescribed minimum standards regarding evidence, injunctions, damages, other remedies, the right to information, the indemnification of the defendant and the administrative procedures.

It is essential for your SME, as an owner of intellectual property rights, to know that the judicial authorities in a large number of countries have the power to order rapid and effective interim measures, aimed at putting an end to an alleged infringement. .

In order to prevent the import of counterfeit branded goods and pirated goods, (international) border measures can be implemented in many countries by the customs administration. As a holder of intellectual property rights, your SME can be helped more easily at the border by customs officials; because otherwise it will have to tackle more offenders once the products have been distributed in the country.

For more information on the TRIPS Agreement, see the following address:

VSHOW TO ENFORCE THE INTELLECTUAL PROPERTY RIGHTS OF YOURSME?

It is always useful, and often necessary, to seek specialist advice after establishing an infringement of your intellectual property rights.

In order to avoid committing your SME's limited financial and human resources to legal proceedings, once you have established an infringement of your SME's intellectual property rights, you should first consider sending a letter (commonly called “cessation order”) to the author of the alleged infringement to inform him of the possible existence of a dispute between the intellectual property rights of your SME and its commercial activity (indicating exactly the point in dispute) and suggest discussing a possible solution to the problem.

It is advisable to consult a lawyer to draft the "cessation order", in order to avoid the launch, by the alleged infringer, of legal proceedings to assert that no infringement has taken place. place or is about to be worn. This procedure is effective in the event of unintentional infringement, since the offender will either cease its activities or agree to negotiate a license agreement.

When faced with intentional infringement, including but not limited to counterfeiting and piracy, you are strongly advised to seek the assistance of law enforcement authorities to catch the infringer within business premises in order to avoid a breach and to preserve evidence of the alleged breach. In addition, the offender may be obliged by the competent judicial authorities to inform you of the identity of the third parties involved in the production and distribution of the products or services infringing your rights and their distribution channels. As a deterrent, the judicial authorities may order, at the request of your SME,

If, for any reason, your SME wishes to avoid legal proceedings, you may consider using alternative dispute resolution mechanisms such as arbitration or mediation (see the section "Arbitration and mediation").

HASOTHER RELATED LINKS AND DOCUMENTS

"The role of governmental authorities in the enforcement of intellectual property rights" (see document WIPO/IPR/JU/BEY/99/5B available in Adobe PDF format)
By clicking on this link, you can access the following WTO documents (the term "Member" refers to a member of the World Trade Organization, i.e., most often, the name of the country in question)

APPENDIX

GCOLLECTIVE MANAGEMENT OF THE RIGHT'AUTHOR AND RELATED RIGHTS

Before defining this concept of collective management and addressing its main characteristics, let us briefly specify what the notions of copyright and related rights cover.

What is copyright?

When a person creates a literary, musical, scientific or artistic work, he is the owner of this work and decides freely on its use. This person (called "creator" or "author" or even "rights holder") controls the future of the work. Given that under the law the work is protected by copyright from its birth, no formality, such as registration or deposit, is required to ensure this protection. Simple ideas as such are not protected, only the way in which they are expressed.

Copyright is the legal protection conferred on the holder of rights to the original work that he has created. It includes two main categories of rights: economic rights and moral rights.

Economic rights are the rights of reproduction, broadcasting, public performance or interpretation, adaptation, translation, public recitation, public performance, distribution, etc. Moral rights include the right of the author to oppose any deformation, mutilation or other modification of his work which is likely to be prejudicial to his honor or his reputation.

Both categories of rights belong to the creator, who can exercise them freely. By exercise of rights, we mean the right of the creator to use the work himself, to authorize someone else to use it or to prohibit its use by third parties. The fundamental principle underlying copyright is that protected works cannot be used without the permission of the rights holder. However, some national laws provide for limited exceptions to this general rule. In principle, the term of protection extends to the life of the author plus a minimum of 50 years after his death.

These legal aspects are stipulated in international conventions to which most countries are currently parties. Upon accession, Member States should have national legislation in line with international standards.

Internationally, it is the Berne Convention for the Protection of Literary and Artistic Works, commonly known as the "Berne Convention", which confers economic and moral rights. This convention, adopted in 1886, has been revised several times to take account of the impact of new techniques on the level of protection it provides. It is administered by the World Intellectual Property Organization (WIPO), one of the specialized international institutions of the United Nations system.

What is related rights protection?

While the rights conferred by copyright apply to authors, "related rights", also called "neighboring rights", concern other categories of rights holders, namely performers, producers phonograms and broadcasting organizations.

Related rights are the rights that belong to performers, producers of phonograms and broadcasting organizations in relation to their performances, phonograms and broadcasts, respectively.

Related rights differ from copyright in that they belong to holders considered as intermediaries in the production, recording or distribution of works. The link with copyright exists because the three categories of holders of related rights function as auxiliaries in the process of intellectual creation by assisting the authors of works in communicating them to the public. A musician performs a musical work written by a composer; an actor performs a role in a play written by a playwright; phonogram producers, in other words "the recording industry", record and produce songs and music written by authors and composers, played by musicians and sung by artists; broadcasting organizations broadcast works and phonograms from their broadcasting stations.

Internationally, it is the International Convention for the Protection of Performers, Producers of Phonograms and Broadcasting Organizations, better known as the "Rome Convention", which confers related rights. This convention was adopted in 1961 and has not been revised since. It is jointly administered by the United Nations Educational, Scientific and Cultural Organization (UNESCO), the International Labor Organization (ILO) and WIPO.

The 1994 Agreement on Trade-Related Aspects of Intellectual Property Rights (or TRIPS Agreement) incorporates or refers to this international protection.

There are other international treaties relating to copyright and related rights protection. Further information on this subject can be obtained from WIPO (see address on last page).

What is Collective Management of Copyright and Related Rights?

As indicated above, the creator of a work has the right to authorize or prohibit the use of his works. A playwright may agree to have his work performed on stage under certain agreed conditions. A writer can negotiate a contract with a publisher for the publication and distribution of a book. A composer or a musician can accept that his music or his interpretation be recorded on compact disc. These examples show how rights holders can exercise their rights personally.

In other cases, practical reasons prevent, so to speak, the individual exercise of rights with regard to certain types of use. An author is materially incapable of controlling all uses of his works; for example, he is not in a position to contact all the radio or television stations to negotiate the licenses and remuneration relating to the use of his works. Similarly, it is impossible for a broadcasting organization to seek express permission from all authors for the use of all copyrighted works. On average, a television channel broadcasts 60,000 musical works each year; it would therefore be necessary to contact thousands of rights holders to obtain their authorization.
The practical impossibility in which both rightholders and users find themselves to manage these activities individually, makes collective management organizations necessary, whose mission is to bring users and rightholders closer together, especially in these key sectors.

Collective management is the exercise of copyright and related rights by organizations that act in the interest and on behalf of rights holders.

Why is it necessary to collectively manage copyright and related rights?

Composers, writers, musicians, singers, artists and other talented individuals are one of the main riches of a country. Their creative genius enriches our cultural life. To develop their talents and encourage them to create, we must motivate these people, in particular by remunerating them in exchange for the authorization to use their works.

Collective management organizations are an important link between creators and users of copyrighted works (e.g. radio stations) as they guarantee the creators as rightsholders remuneration for the use of their works.

Who are the members?

All owners of copyright or related rights, whether authors, composers, publishers, writers, photographers, musicians or performers, can become members of a collective management organization. Broadcasters are not included in this list as they are considered users, although they have certain rights to their broadcasts. When joining a CMO, members provide certain personal information and declare the works they have created. The information provided forms an integral part of the CMO's documentation and enables the CMO to establish the link between the use of the works and the remuneration for this use and to ensure that the payment ends up at the right address. The works declared by the members of the organization constitute what is commonly called the "national" or "local" repertoire (as opposed to the international repertoire, which is made up of foreign works managed by collective management organizations around the world).

What are the most common rights that are managed collectively?

The rights most commonly managed by collective management organizations include:

The right of public performance (music played or performed in discos, restaurants and other public places);

The right to broadcast (live and based on performances recorded on radio and television);

Mechanical reproduction rights of musical works (the reproduction of works on compact disc, tape, vinyl disc, cassette, minidisc or other recording medium);

The rights to interpret or perform dramatic works (plays);

The right of reprographic reproduction of literary and musical works (photocopying);

Related rights (rights to remuneration of performers and producers of phonograms for the broadcasting or communication to the public of their phonograms).

How does collective management work?

There are various types of collective management organizations or groupings of organizations, depending on the categories of works concerned (music, dramatic works, multimedia productions, etc.), which collectively manage various types of rights.

First, there are the "traditional" CMOs. They act on behalf of their members, negotiate tariffs and terms of use with users, issue authorizations for use, and collect and distribute royalties. The rights holder is not directly involved in any of these activities.

Rights clearance centers deliver licenses to users which reflect the conditions of use of works and the terms of remuneration set individually by each of the rightholders who are members of the center (in the field of reprography, for example, authors written works such as books, magazines and other periodicals). In this case, the center fulfills the functions of an agent for the rights holder who takes a direct part in the management by fixing the methods of use of his works.

"One-Stop-Shops" are a kind of alliance of different Collective Management Organizations that offer users a centralized source to obtain permissions easily and quickly. There is currently an increased tendency to set up organizations of this type, given the growing popularity of multimedia productions (productions composed or created from several categories of works, including computer software) which require a multitude of different permissions.

IN THE FIELD OF MUSICAL WORKS(encompassing all types of music - modern, jazz, classical, symphonic, blues and pop - both instrumental and vocal), documentation, licensing and distribution are the three pillars on which the collective management of public performance and broadcasting rights.

The collective management organization negotiates with users (such as radio or television stations, discos, cinemas, restaurants, etc.) or user groups and authorizes them to use works from its repertoire which are protected by the copyright against payment and under certain conditions. On the basis of its documentation (information on members and their works) and programs submitted by users (for example, records of music played on the radio), the collective management organization distributes the copyright royalties among its members in accordance with pre-established distribution rules. In general, an amount intended to cover administrative costs and, in certain countries, to finance promotional activities in the socio-cultural field, is deducted from copyright royalties. The royalties actually paid to copyright holders correspond to the use of their works and are accompanied by a statement of uses. These activities and operations are carried out using software packages specially designed for this purpose.

IN THE FIELD OF DRAMATIC WORKS(which include scripts, screenplays, mime shows, ballets, plays, operas and musicals), collective management is practiced in a different way in that the collective management organization operates as an agent on behalf of the authors. It negotiates with the organizations representing the theaters a contract which stipulates the minimum conditions of exploitation of each work.

In addition, the interpretation of each play requires the authorization of the author, in the form of an individual contract specifying the specific conditions imposed by the author.
The collective management organization then announces that the authorization has been given by the author concerned and collects the corresponding remuneration.

IN THE FIELD OF PRINTED WORKS(i.e. books, magazines and other periodicals, newspapers, reports and song texts), collective management boils down to the granting of the right of reprographic reproduction, in other words, to the authorization of photocopy protected material given to institutions such as libraries, public bodies, universities, schools and consumer associations. To the extent permitted by international conventions, national laws may provide for non-voluntary license systems. In this case, the right of use against remuneration is granted without it being necessary to obtain the consent of the holder of the rights. Remuneration is administered by Collective Management Organizations. In the particular case of reproduction for private and personal purposes, certain national laws contain specific provisions providing for the payment of equitable remuneration to the rightholders; this is financed by levying a fee on equipment or photocopies, or both.

IN THE FIELD OF RELATED RIGHTS, the laws of some countries provide for a right to remuneration, a royalty to be paid to performers or producers of phonograms, or both, as soon as a commercial sound recording is communicated to the public or used for broadcasting. Royalties of this type of use are collected and distributed, either by an organization set up jointly by the performers and the producers of phonograms, or by separate organizations, depending on the relationship between the interested parties and depending of the legal system of the country.

What is the scope of CMOs?

National laws recognizing rights in literary and artistic works and related rights have effect only within the territory of the country concerned. In accordance with the principle of national treatment enshrined in both the Berne Convention and the Rome Convention, foreign rights holders are treated, in almost all respects, the same as nationals of a country. This principle is defended by collective management organizations which, under reciprocal representation contracts, administer foreign repertoires on their national territory, exchange information and pay royalties to foreign rights holders.

Links with non-governmental organizations

At present, there is a well-established global network of collective management organizations and these are strongly represented by non-governmental organizations such as the International Confederation of Societies of Authors and Composers (CISAC), the International Federation of Managing Reproduction Rights (IFRRO) and, at European level, the Association of European Performers' Organizations (AEPO), to mention but a few.

As part of its international development cooperation activities, WIPO works closely with the above-mentioned organizations, as well as others such as the International Federation of Actors (FIA), the International Federation of Musicians (FIM) or the International Federation of the Phonographic Industry (IFPI).
The objective is to help developing countries which so request to create collective management organizations and to strengthen the dynamism and effectiveness of existing organizations in order to enable them, among other things, to meet the challenges of digital environment. WIPO carries out such activities as part of its development cooperation program.

The socio-economic and cultural dimension

Collective management renders eminent services to the world of music and to other creative arts. By managing their rights, the system rewards creators for their work and, in turn, creators are more motivated to develop and employ their talents in an environment that affords them adequate copyright and related rights protection. and offers them an effective system for managing their rights. Such a situation encourages creators to contribute to the development of the cultural sector, attracts foreign investment and, in general, allows the public to benefit from a wide range of works. Taken together, these factors have undeniable effects on the economies of countries. Cultural industries provide up to 6% of the gross national product of certain large countries; income from the collective management of copyright and related rights represents a substantial part of this percentage.

Some collective management organizations offer all kinds of social benefits to their members. Often they help pay medical bills or insurance premiums, pay a pension or some form of guaranteed income based on a member's royalty history.

Some CMOs also sponsor cultural activities to promote the national repertoire of works inside and outside the country. They encourage the organization of theater festivals, musical competitions, productions of national folklore and musical anthologies and other similar activities.

Social benefits and the promotion of cultural activities are not compulsory. However, when they are foreseen, they can be financed by means of a deduction operated by the collective management organization on the royalties which it collects. The idea of a deduction, which, according to CISAC rules, should not exceed 10% of net receipts, is not unanimous among collective management organisations.

Collective management in the digital environment

Works protected by copyright will increasingly be communicated in digital form, via global networks such as the Internet. Consequently, the collective management of copyright and related rights by public, semi-public and private entities will be reorganized in such a way as to take advantage of the efficiency gains resulting from information technology. The ever-increasing possibilities offered to rightsholders by the Internet, at the same time as the advent of multimedia productions, have repercussions on the methods of protection, exercise and management of copyright and related rights and, also, on the enforcement of these rights.

In the online world of the new millennium, rights management acquires a new dimension. Today, protected works are digitized, compressed, downloaded, copied and distributed via the Internet to all corners of the world. The growing power of this network makes it possible to store and deliver masses of protected material online. It is already possible to download the content of a book or listen to music and record it from cyberspace. The result is unlimited opportunities, but also many challenges for rightholders, users and collective management organisations.

Many collective management organizations have created systems for the online provision of information on the assignment of works and content, the monitoring of uses and the collection and distribution of royalties for different categories of works under the digital environment. These digital information systems, which depend on the development of unique numbering systems and codes, inserted into digital media such as compact discs and films, allow the correct identification of works, rights holders, media themselves together with the provision of other relevant information. Adequate legal protection is required in order to prevent acts aimed at circumventing technical protection measures and, also,

In 1996, two treaties were concluded under the auspices of WIPO to address the challenges of protecting and managing copyright and related rights in the digital age. Known as the "Internet Treaties", the WIPO Copyright Treaty and the WIPO Performances and Phonograms Treaty (WCT and WPPT respectively - see the WIPO information brochures on them) deal, inter alia, with obligations relating to technical protection measures and information on the management of rights in the digital environment. They guarantee rights holders protection when their works are disseminated on the Internet; they also contain provisions obliging the national legislator to provide effective protection of technological measures by prohibiting the import, manufacture and distribution of illicit instruments or materials designed to circumvent technical protection measures and by declaring illegal any act that undermines rights management information systems.

There are other brochures devoted to copyright, related rights and the WCT and WPPT treaties. WIPO provides them on request. Readers who would like additional information on collective management can contact WIPO's Copyright Collective Management Division at +41-22 338 91 43 (secretariat), or visit the website WIPO website at:

www.ingramcontent.com/pod-product-compliance
Lightning Source LLC
LaVergne TN
LVHW080555160826
845677LV00010B/1857
* 9 7 9 8 8 4 8 7 7 0 4 8 3 *